A Trainer's Guide

to

Caring for Children in Family Child Care

Diane Trister Dodge
Derry G. Koralek
Debra D. Foulks

Cover design by
Jennifer Barrett

Teaching
Strategies®Inc.
Washington, DC

Published by

Teaching Strategies, Inc.
P.O. Box 42243
Washington, DC 20015

Third Printing: 2005

ISBN: 1-879537-11-7

Library of Congress Catalog Number: 93-061834

Acknowledgments

A Trainer's Guide to Caring for Children in Family Child Care draws much of its content and format from other resources developed by Teaching Strategies, particularly the guides for trainers implementing *Caring for Infants and Toddlers* and *Caring for Preschool Children*. For their contributions to these materials we thank Catherine Ann New, Amy Laura Dombro, Abbey Griffin, Elisabeth Hudgins, David Riley, and Peter Pizzolongo. The chapters on One-on-One Training/Mentoring and Assessing Each Provider's Progress are based on *A Trainer's Guide to the Family Child Care Providers' Training Program* we developed under a contract with the U.S. Army Child Development Services. For their guidance and support throughout this project, we are indebted to M.-A. Lucas, Chief, Army Child and Youth Services, and Patricia Kasold, who served as Army Family Child Care Program Manager during this contract.

Two new chapters were developed specifically for this *Trainer's Guide:* Supporting Providers' Professional Development and Conducting Group Training Sessions. They emphasize the importance of ensuring that all training—whether offered in the context of self-instruction, one-on-one mentoring, or as part of courses or ongoing workshops—enhances the professional development and career paths of family child care providers. We wish to acknowledge the assistance of Laura J. Colker and Kerry Harris in the sections describing effective training and the certification and credentialing systems for family child care providers and programs.

We hope that this *Trainer's Guide* will enable resource and referral agencies, colleges and universities, child care and Head Start agencies, vocational/technical schools, and individual trainers to use *Caring for Children in Family Child Care* more effectively and to ensure that it is part of a cohesive system of professional development for family child care providers.

DTD
DGK
DDF

January 1994

Contents

Introduction

This is an exciting and challenging time to be involved professionally in caring for children. It is exciting because, after decades of research, we know that high quality child care programs can make an important difference for children throughout their lives. It is challenging because this knowledge imposes a clear responsibility on our profession to create high quality programs, whether children are cared for in centers or in family child care homes.

Family child care (FCC) is an increasingly important profession. In the United States today, more than 64 percent of the children under age six have mothers who work outside the home, and many of these children go to family child care homes. FCC providers were once almost totally isolated in their homes and viewed as babysitters. Now they are increasingly involved in professional activities that link them with other providers and enable them to enhance their skills and knowledge. Many join professional organizations, attend training sessions and conferences, and earn credentials. They view themselves as professionals and work hard to offer quality services for children and families.

Two key factors in achieving a high quality FCC program are training and support. Child care associations, Head Start programs, resource and referral (R & R) agencies, training organizations, and colleges and universities can play a central role in reaching out to providers. Such organizations offer support networks and training and mentoring programs to help providers achieve their professional goals.

This *Trainer's Guide* shows how *Caring for Children in Family Child Care* can serve as the focus for workshops, courses, or on-site training and mentoring. The 13 modules address the full range of knowledge and skills providers need to offer a quality program for children from birth through age 12. The format and design of the materials make them appropriate for workshops and allow trainers and mentors to individualize their training and support. Workshops can be presented in a series with the goal of preparing providers for seeking a credential or accreditation, or individually over a period of time for the primary purpose of meeting a state's training requirements. Using the modules as a curriculum framework will ensure that the training is part of a meaningful progression of professional development. A provider's skills and knowledge will be enhanced with either approach.

The Guide is written for any individual responsible for overseeing provider training. For the training program to be most effective, trainers or mentors should have a strong foundation in child development from birth through school-age and a broad understanding of the unique characteristics of family child care. Your role is to provide feedback and support as providers complete each of the learning activities.

There are four chapters and seven appendices in the *Trainer's Guide*. Chapter I, Supporting Providers' Professional Development, highlights the meaning of professional development and discusses the standards for professionals who care for children in their homes. It explains how *Caring for Children in Family Child Care* can help providers obtain a Child Development Associate Credential from the Council for Professional Recognition and accreditation for their program from the National Association for Family Child Care. It also shows how modules can be grouped for college courses and suggests the number of clock hours for each module.

Chapter II, Conducting Group Training Sessions, discusses principles of adult learning and shows how they can be applied to planning effective workshops. A sample training outline for group sessions based on one of the modules is included.

Chapter III, One-on-One Training/Mentoring, gives an overview of the role of the trainer or mentor in guiding individual providers through each module, including how to observe and offer feedback through home visits and phone conferences. Charts for each module outline what providers do in the learning activities and the role of trainers or mentors.

Chapter IV, Assessing Each Provider's Progress, explains the assessment process. Knowledge and competency assessments for each module are included.

The Appendices contain forms and resources for implementing *Caring for Children in Family Child Care*. To help you plan group sessions, there is a blank form that follows the sample training outline in Chapter II. To support the assessment process, you will find answer sheets for the knowledge assessments and observation forms for the competency assessments. To document a provider's progress through the modules, you can use the tracking forms, documentation of training hours form, and the certificate of completion.

I. Supporting Providers' Professional Development

I. Supporting Providers' Professional Development

Every profession establishes standards for appropriate practice and a system for credentialing its members and accrediting its programs. Professional organizations such as the National Association for Family Child Care (NAFCC), the National Association for the Education of Young Children (NAEYC), and the Council for Professional Recognition (the Council) have defined standards that guide quality programs and the educators who strive to achieve these standards.

The standards that apply to family child care programs include the following:

- The Family Child Care Accreditation Project, Wheelock College. (2003). *Quality standards for NAFCC accreditation* (Third ed.). Salt Lake City, UT: National Association for Family Child Care. Available at http://www.nafcc.org/books/qual03.pdf

- Copple, C. & Bredekamp, S. (Eds.). (1997). *Developmentally appropriate practice in early childhood programs* (Rev. ed.). Washington, DC: NAEYC. Available at http://www.naeyc.org

- Council for Professional Recognition. (1997; new edition expected in 2005). *The Child Development Associate assessment system and competency standards for family child care providers*. Washington, DC: The Council. Available at http://www.cdacouncil.org/shop/index.html

Family child care (FCC) providers, who may care for children birth through age 12, are considered part of the field of early childhood education and belong to the profession. As defined by NAEYC, the *field* includes anyone who provides early childhood services for young children and families. The *profession* refers to those who have acquired some professional knowledge and who see themselves as on a "professional path."

Defining a Professional Path for Providers

A professional path requires 1) completion of or enrollment in a credit-bearing early childhood professional preparation program that meets recognized guidelines or 2) ongoing participation in formal training that may not be credit bearing but is designed to lead to the acquisition of competency, that could be assessed through mechanisms such as the Child Development Associate (CDA) Credential and/or transformed into credit toward another professional credential or degree.[1]

Educators who offer courses, workshops, or individualized staff development for providers have a special obligation to ensure that these experiences lead to a credential, a degree, and/or accreditation. Too often FCC providers attend training sessions that are scattered, of variable quality, and fail to lead to the advancement of their professional knowledge and skills. In order to ensure that training experiences contribute to a provider's professional path, they must address the profession's definition of core knowledge and apply the principles of effective staff development.

---

[1] National Association for the Education of Young Children. (1994). NAEYC Position statement: A conceptual framework for early childhood professional development. *Young Children, 49*(3), 68-77.

Subject Areas that Define the Core Knowledge

NAEYC and the Council have defined eight subject areas that form the core knowledge of our profession. Early childhood professionals should be able to:[2]

- demonstrate an understanding of child development and apply this knowledge in practice;

- observe and assess children's behavior in planning and individualizing teaching practices and curriculum;

- establish and maintain a safe and healthy environment for children;

- plan and implement developmentally appropriate curriculum that advances all areas of children's learning and development, including social, emotional, intellectual, and physical;

- establish supportive relationships with children and implement developmentally appropriate techniques of guidance and group management;

- establish and maintain positive and productive relationships with families;

- support the development and learning of individual children, recognizing that children are best understood in the context of family, culture, and society; and

- demonstrate an understanding of the early childhood profession and make a commitment to professionalism.

Caring for Children in Family Child Care is one training program that addresses this core knowledge.

Principles of Effective Professional Development

In order to ensure that training experiences are effective and meaningful for providers, they should be planned according to accepted principles for staff development. As defined by NAEYC,[3] effective professional development experiences:

- are part of an ongoing process allowing providers to continually incorporate and apply new knowledge and skills related to working with children and families;

- are grounded in a sound theoretical and philosophical base and structured as a coherent and systematic program;

- are responsive to an individual's background, experiences, and current role;

- allow providers to see clear linkages between theory and practice;

- use interactive, hands-on approaches that encourage providers to learn from one another;

---

[2] Ibid.
[3] Ibid.

- contribute to positive self-esteem by acknowledging the skills and resources providers bring to the training process;

- provide opportunities for application and reflection and allow providers to be observed and receive feedback about what they have learned; and

- encourage providers to take responsibility for planning their own professional development program.

When FCC providers attend workshops, participate in one-on-one training, or take college courses to improve their knowledge and skills, these professional development experiences should lead to a credential or accreditation. A primary incentive for providers to participate in and complete a training program is the recognition that comes with the achievement of a credential and/or accreditation from a professional organization.

While there are a variety of credentialing and accreditation programs, the two most widely known are the Council's CDA Credential and the NAFCC Accreditation.

The Process for Obtaining a CDA Credential

The Child Development Associate National Credentialing Program is a major effort to provide early childhood educators with a credential based on demonstrated competency. The program began in 1971 with the goal of enhancing the quality of early childhood education by improving, evaluating, and recognizing the competence of individuals who work with children from birth to age five in center-based and family child care settings.

The Council for Professional Recognition establishes the policies and sets the standards for the credentialing program, and awards the CDA Credential to adults who demonstrate competence in caring for young children. To date, nearly 85,000 early care and education workers have received a CDA Credential. A candidate must be able to demonstrate the knowledge and skills outlined in the Competency Standards. These standards are divided into six **competency goals** and further defined in 13 **functional areas**.

CDA Competency Goals and Functional Areas*	
Competency Goals	**Functional Areas**
I. To establish and maintain a safe, healthy learning environment	1. **Safe:** Candidate provides a safe environment to prevent and reduce injuries.
	2. **Healthy:** Candidate promotes good health and nutrition and provides an environment that contributes to the prevention of illness.
	3. **Learning Environment:** Candidate uses space, relationships, materials, and routines as resources for constructing an interesting, secure, and enjoyable environment that encourages play, exploration, and learning.

* Reprinted with permission from The Council for Professional Recognition. (1997). *The Child Development Associate assessment system and competency standards for family child care providers*. Washington, DC: The Council.

II.	**To advance physical and intellectual competence**	**4.**	**Physical:** Candidate provides a variety of equipment, activities, and opportunities to promote the physical development of children.
		5.	**Cognitive:** Candidate provides activities and opportunities that encourage curiosity, exploration, and problem-solving appropriate to the developmental levels and learning styles of children.
		6.	**Communication:** Candidate actively communicates with children and provides opportunities and support for children to understand, acquire, and use verbal and nonverbal means of communicating thoughts and feelings.
		7.	**Creative:** Candidate provides opportunities that stimulate children to play with sound, rhythm, language, materials, space, and ideas in individual ways and to express their creative abilities.
III.	**To support social and emotional development and provide positive guidance**	**8.**	**Self:** Candidate provides physical and emotional security for each child and helps each child know, accept, and take pride in himself or herself and to develop a sense of independence.
		9.	**Social:** Candidate helps each child feel accepted in the group, helps children learn to communicate and get along with others, and encourages feelings of empathy and mutual respect among children and adults.
		10.	**Guidance:** Candidate provides a supportive environment in which children can begin to learn and practice appropriate and acceptable behaviors as individuals and as a group.
IV.	**To establish positive and productive relationships with families**	**11.**	**Families:** Candidate maintains an open, friendly, and cooperative relationship with each child's family, encourages their involvement in the program, and supports the child's relationship with his or her family.
V.	**To ensure a well-run, purposeful program responsive to participant needs**	**12.**	**Program Management:** Candidate is a manager who uses all available resources to ensure an effective operation. The Candidate is a competent organizer, planner, record keeper, communicator, and cooperative coworker.
VI.	**To maintain a commitment to professionalism**	**13.**	**Professionalism:** Candidate makes decisions based on knowledge of early childhood theories and practices. The Candidate promotes quality in child care services. The Candidate takes advantage of opportunities to improve competence, both for personal and professional growth and for the benefit of children and families.

There are two routes to obtaining a CDA Credential: Direct Assessment and the Professional Preparation Program (also known as CDA P$_3$). In addition, providers already certified in one setting (family child care, home visiting, or center-based care for preschoolers or infants and toddlers) can become credentialed in another. To stay current on the process for obtaining a CDA Credential, contact The Council for Professional Recognition at www.cdacouncil.org or 800-424-4310.

Direct Assessment

To apply through Direct Assessment, a provider must document completion of 120 contact hours of training with no less than ten hours in each of the eight subject areas defined by the profession. Formal training can be provided by training specialists, Head Start or child care agencies, colleges, vocational/technical schools, U.S. or state government agencies, the U.S. Military Service, organizations for family child care providers, or resource and referral agencies, and must cover the specific subject areas outlined by the Council.

Completion of the 13 modules in *Caring for Children in Family Child Care* enables providers to meet or exceed the Council's training requirements. Providers spend approximately three hours a week working on the learning activities in the 13 modules. Time spent in workshops, courses, or one-on-one mentoring around the learning activities in *Caring for Children in Family Child Care* should be documented in order to verify all contact hours. (See Appendix E for a sample form for documenting contact hours.)

Providers are responsible for developing a Professional Resource File, which is a collection of documents to use in working with children and families. The learning activities in *Caring for Children in Family Child Care* include many opportunities for providers to document work and collect materials that can be included in their Professional Resource File.

Direct Assessment also requires providers to complete a written and oral assessment and be observed working directly with children. The knowledge and competency assessments used after completing each module will help providers prepare for the CDA assessments.

Professional Preparation Program

In the second route to obtaining a CDA Credential, the Council will arrange for providers to enter a college-level Professional Preparation Program, which offers training and assessment using the Council's curriculum, *Essentials for Child Development Associates*. There are three phases in the CDA Professional Preparation Program: field work, instructional course work, and evaluation.

CDA Advisors and seminar instructors can use the learning activities in *Caring for Children in Family Child Care* to supplement those suggested in the Council's curriculum. The learning activities for each module can enhance a provider's Professional Resource File. The overview vignettes, self-assessments, and readings in each module also provide a wealth of ideas and information for course discussions. The suggestions for supporting providers and extending learning for each module (found in Chapter III of the *Trainer's Guide*) provide other ways to increase a provider's understanding of the CDA subject areas. Finally, the knowledge assessments can be useful practice for candidates preparing for the written evaluation.

The Process for Obtaining NAFCC Accreditation

FCC providers who participate in the *Caring for Children in Family Child Care* training program will be enhancing their own programs in ways that also address the NAFCC accreditation criteria. The NAFCC accreditation process—which combines self-study, informal and formal training, a parent survey, and an onsite FCC home and provider evaluation by a Qualified Observer—is coordinated by the applicant with some assistance from NAFCC. Overall completion time varies from 9 months (the mandated minimum) to 3 years. The provider's previous experience and available time and educational resources will affect the total time required. NAFCC formally trains all Qualified Observers and sponsors their FCC home visits.

The sequence of accreditation events begins when providers receive an application from, and return it to, NAFCC (along with half-payment). Next, the provider works through the NAFCC Self-Study Workbook and administers a parental survey to identify areas requiring future education, training, or program changes. Finally, after the provider has followed up with all necessary actions, he or she re-contacts NAFCC (and sends the remaining half-payment) to request and complete "a formal self-evaluation" and arrange the onsite observation. Accreditation is granted (or withheld, pending further improvements) in writing from the NAFCC Accreditation Commission.

To stay current on the process for obtaining an NAFCC Accreditation, contact NAFCC at www.nafcc.org or 801-269-9338.

NAFCC QUALITY STANDARDS[4]

Relationships

Warm, responsive relationships help children develop to their full potential. Open communications and mutual respect help providers partner with parents for the best interest of the children.

Environment

The home is welcoming, safe, and comfortable, offering materials and equipment that are appropriate for the children in care and support activities across all the domains of development.

Activities

As the provider observes children's activities and interests, s/he supports and extends their play and offers new activities and materials to build upon their learning.

Developmental Learning Goals

Children learn to get along well with each other, feel secure in their own identity, and build competency across a wide range of areas. In addition to social and self development, these include physical development, cognition and language, literacy and math development, and creativity. The provider supports children's play, offers planned activities, and builds on spontaneous opportunities to support the learning goals.

Safety and Health

Children's physical well-being is supported through careful supervision, preparation for emergencies, minimizing the spread of disease, and serving of nutritious food.

Professional and Business Practices

The provider follows sound, ethical business practices, pursues continuing education and training, and seeks support from others when needed.

---

[4] National Association for Family Child Care. *NAFCC Accreditation Brochure,* Web Version. Salt Lake City, UT: Author. Retrieved May 5, 2004, from http://www.nafcc.org/accred/brochure.html

Making Training Count

Whether formal training is required as in obtaining a CDA, or recommended, as in securing program accreditation through NAFCC, it is important to ensure that all training experiences contribute to a provider's professional path. This means that professional development experiences:

- are offered by a trainer who has a background and experience in early childhood education;

- are conducted by an agency that is qualified to offer training (such as resource and referral agencies, vocational/technical schools, colleges, universities, child care, and Head Start associations);

- address one or more of the CDA subject areas and/or the criteria in the *Quality Standards for NAFCC Accreditation*;

- are documented and certified.

There are several ways to document a provider's participation in training including college transcripts, certificates, or documentation forms like the one found in Appendix E. Some states have specific requirements for the content, hours, and documentation of training. It is important to ensure that professional development experiences address these requirements.

The chart on the following page illustrates how the 13 modules in *Caring for Children in Family Child Care* could be applied to obtaining a CDA Credential or NAFCC Accreditation. The modules are grouped to illustrate how they might be organized into college courses. This model is based on 12 credit hours that would lead to fulfillment of the requirements for a credential, accreditation, or college credit. Another way that colleges might award credit is to offer a series of one-credit-hour classes based on the modules, thus giving providers a range of choices for augmenting their training experiences.

Course Title	Modules Covered	Suggested Clock Hours Per Module	CDA Subject Area Addressed	NAFCC Accreditation Assessment Profile
Establishing the Environment	Module 1-Safe Module 2-Healthy Module 3-Learning Environment	12 12 14	Planning a safe, healthy, learning environment	Safety and Health, Nutrition, Environment
Child Growth and Development: Cognitive and Physical	Module 4-Physical Module 5-Cognitive Module 6-Communication Module 7-Creative	10 10 10 10	Steps to advance children's physical and intellectual development Principles of child development and learning	Relationships, Developmental Learning Goals, Activities
Child Growth and Development: Social and Emotional	Module 8-Self Module 9-Social Module 10-Guidance	11 11 16	Positive ways to support children's social and emotional development Principles of child development and learning	Relationships, Developmental Learning Goals, Activities
Introduction to the Early Childhood Profession	Module 11-Families Module 12-Program Management Module 13-Professionalism	10 20 10	Strategies to establish productive relationships with families Strategies to manage an effective program operation Maintaining a commitment to professionalism Observing and documenting children's behavior	Professional and Business Practices
Applied Early Childhood Practices (Lab or Practicum)	This course would include the instructor or mentor observing a student's application of material presented in class and providing individualized support and feedback.	16	Observations by an Advisor are part of the CDA credentialing process.	Observation by a Qualified Observer is part of the NAFCC credentialing process.

When using the modules for courses or group training sessions, you might include observation visits in a provider's home as a component of the training program. If you are teaching a college course, observation visits can be established as a lab or practicum. Although 13 observation visits are considered ideal (one per module), a minimum of four is recommended when using these materials as part of group training: one visit following completion of each course on the chart. Visits can be supplemented with telephone conversations to discuss the learning activities in each module. These conversations allow you and the provider to discuss how the material learned can be applied in the FCC home and to celebrate the provider's successes. The Module Feedback Schedule in Chapter III shows one way to organize feedback when using this program for one-on-one training. You can adapt this schedule, or develop your own, to ensure that ongoing, individualized support is included when using this program in a group setting.

II. Conducting Group Training Sessions

II. Conducting Group Training Sessions

While *Caring for Children in Family Child Care* is designed to be a supervised, self-instructional training program, it can also serve as the focus for a series of workshops or as the textbook for college courses.

This chapter offers suggestions on planning training sessions that are based on principles of adult learning. It emphasizes the importance of logistics, describes how to introduce training to providers, and identifies a variety of effective training techniques. A sample training outline for Module 10: Guidance is included to illustrate how the learning activities can serve as the focus for group sessions.

Attending to Logistics

No matter what the topic, training is most successful when it is well planned. Simple details can make or break a workshop. Attention to logistics is worth the time you invest. Listed below are some general pointers that will help you ensure everyone's comfort.

- Schedule training sessions at times that will be convenient for providers—for example, on Saturday mornings or, if applicable, on prearranged "in-service" days. Providers have steady demands on their time, both professionally and personally. By accommodating their schedules, you are not just being courteous; you increase the possibility of high attendance.

- Arrange for child care at the training site. Since many providers have children of their own, advertising the availability of this service can eliminate a possible obstacle to attendance.

- Provide advance confirmation of the training date and time and written instructions for finding the building and the room where training is to be held.

- Provide snacks for both trainees and the children being cared for. By letting participants know in advance that food and drink are available, you eliminate another deterrent to attendance. A snack break will also refresh minds and energize participants.

- Make sure that all materials and equipment needed for training have been arranged for or prepared in advance. This includes audiovisual equipment and supplies, chart paper, markers, tape, chalk, handouts, and evaluation sheets. Ensure that all equipment is in working order with the necessary replacement bulbs, extension cords, and adapters on hand.

- Check that the training room is comfortable before the start of training. Chairs need to be roomy enough for participants to sit for a long period of time without getting restless. Participants will also need something to write on (other than their laps). The room temperature should be appropriate, and air should be circulating freely. An overheated room can put an audience to sleep quickly.

- Arrange furniture to suit your working style. Most trainers prefer circles, semi-circles, or small groups of tables. As a general rule, training is best received when the room is informally arranged to allow for interaction between providers.

- Display name tags, sign-in sheets, agendas, and reference materials in areas that are readily accessible to participants.

- Greet participants when they enter the training room. If this is not possible, arrange for someone else associated with the training to do so. By individually welcoming providers, you'll set them at ease.

- At the outset, let participants know the rules that will be in effect. If, for example, a "no smoking" rule is imposed, participants should be advised about areas where smoking is permitted during breaks.

- Before beginning, point out the location of rest rooms, telephones, and water fountains. This will minimize interruptions once training starts.

By attending to these few logistical concerns, you'll find that the content of the training program will be the focus of your attention—not scrambling for extension cords or searching for engineers to turn up the heat. Preparation goes a long way when it comes to training.

Basing Training on Principles of Adult Learning

In planning training on *Caring for Children in Family Child Care*—or any subject, for that matter—it's important to reflect on what we know about how adults learn. There are several principles of adult learning theory that can guide you as you plan your training program.

- Adults bring a wealth of previous experiences to training.

- Adults perceive their own experiences as unique and private. They are not always comfortable or willing to share these experiences with a group.

- For adults, time is valuable. They need to be convinced that their time will not be wasted at a training session.

- Adults are self-directed. They like to retain control of the learning experience.

- Adults learn in a variety of ways and styles, but methods in which the adult learner actively participates—in addition to watching and listening—are preferred by the majority of adults.

- Motivation for learning is closely related to the perceived immediate utility of the information being taught.

In applying these tenets of adult education to your training program, consider using these techniques.[5]

- Share the specific training goals and objectives with participants. Effective training involves developing a shared group commitment to goals and objectives.

- Draw on participants' experiences. Training becomes more meaningful when participants relate concepts to personal situations and experiences.

- Establish from the beginning that participants are responsible for their own learning. It is important to state at the outset that everyone will take something different from the session, depending on what is important to them, how much effort they put into the session, and whether they integrate and use what they learn.

- Emphasize the development of skills rather than the rote learning of responses. Learning involved assimilating new information and using it to improve skills.

- Encourage trainees' active involvement. Role playing, small group analysis, discussion, and case studies help participants apply training concepts, principles, and strategies to life situations.

- Encourage trainees to make interpretations and draw conclusions. Trainers should provide the background information, data, and examples needed to help the group identify patterns or trends, make generalizations, and draw conclusions.

- Plan a balance of different types of activities using a variety of instructional media. A balance of approaches contributes to the group's interest and ultimately ensures greater retention and application of skills and content.

Introducing Training to Providers

For some providers, training will be a new experience. Even an experienced FCC provider may feel shy about talking aloud in a group, sharing experiences and ideas, or asking questions. As a trainer, one of your most important functions is to help participants feel comfortable about expressing their views. Here are some ideas you might try to help providers feel more comfortable during training.

- Acknowledge that sharing ideas and experiences in a group may feel a little uncomfortable at first.

- Underscore the importance of training for the provider. Stress that the purpose of training is to help providers do their jobs better.

- Encourage providers to express their opinions. Emphasize that everyone's views are valuable and that there is usually more than one correct way to approach a topic.

---

[5] Diane Trister Dodge, Derry Gosselin Koralek, and Peter J. Pizzolongo, *A Guide for Education Coordinators in Head Start* (Washington, DC: U.S. Department of Health and Human Services, 1986), pp. 169-170.

- Look for nonverbal cues that will alert you to the fact that someone may be uncomfortable with the subject matter being discussed (squirming), shy about contributing (avoiding gaze), or angry (turning away with the entire body). Then try to respond to what you see.

- Ask questions appropriately in response to cues you receive from the audience. At times, both direct questions ("What books do you think would be helpful to a child whose parents are divorcing?") and open-ended questions ("How would you handle that situation?") are needed. Also, refer a question to the entire group if you sense that an in-depth discussion would be beneficial. ("That's a tough problem. Does anyone have a suggestion?")

- Don't embarrass participants by pressuring each person to contribute.

- If conflicts or disagreements occur, guide the discussion to encourage compromise or at least acceptance of conflicting points of view.

- Use small-group activities as opportunities to discuss feelings, either through role-playing, simulations, or problem-solving assignments.

- Encourage participants to be active listeners as well as active discussants.

- Be available to discuss issues and topics with participants during breaks. Some providers may be more comfortable sharing their views with you on a one-on-one basis rather than in front of the whole group.

Selecting Training Techniques

To a large extent the choice of training techniques depends on a trainer's personal preferences and philosophy of training. For example, if you're a skilled lecturer, you will want to include mini-lectures as part of your workshops. On the other hand, if you're uncomfortable as a lecturer, you may rely on small-group activities. Your choice of techniques will also reflect the preferences of those whom you are training. This means selecting a variety of approaches and methods that suit your style and meet the different learning styles of the providers you will be training.

The training techniques listed here are a potpourri of ideas. Some of these techniques will be perfect for you; others will not. Try out as many techniques as possible to find those that suit you. You'll find that nearly all these techniques can be modified and reshaped to accommodate both your needs and the needs of the groups you'll be training.

Handouts

Written material such as articles from professional journals can be used as background reading or to provide further illustration of content covered in the learning activities. You might wish to use written materials as content summaries, as training assignments, or as supplemental readings for interested participants. Be sure to get permission from copyright holders before reproducing and distributing materials that you do not write yourself.

Audiovisuals

Audiovisuals can be very effective training tools. Videotapes such as *Caring and Learning* (available from Teaching Strategies) show realistic and relevant scenes from four family child care homes. Slides you take of providers' programs would also be a good way to share some of the ideas you discover in your home visits. Audiovisual resources allow you to reinforce good practices and enable providers to learn more about each other.

Overheads

Overhead transparencies break up the monotony of the spoken voice and reinforce for participants the key points of a lecture. Here are some suggestions for developing transparencies.

- Include key words and phrases only.

- Use large printed letters so that the overhead can be read from any point in the room.

- Be sure that the contrast between the background color and lettering is sufficient for easy reading.

- Keep illustrations (if any) simple.

- Graphs, if used, should be simple and readily understood.

Problem-Solving Activities

One of the most popular and effective training techniques is group problem-solving. Brainstorming solutions to realistic problems energizes a group and generates useful ideas. The theory behind brainstorming is to separate idea creation from idea evaluation. It works best in groups of 5 to 12; a recorder and a moderator are needed. Here are the rules for brainstorming.

- All ideas are listed; no critical remarks are allowed.

- "Hitchhiking" is permissible—if one participant can improve upon or combine previously mentioned ideas, so much the better.

- "Freewheeling" is encouraged—even outlandish ideas keep the group momentum going.

- The more, the better—the more ideas generated, the more likely there will be some viable solutions among these ideas.

- Evaluation comes only after all ideas have been generated.

To illustrate how this technique works, consider asking participants to brainstorm any of the following topics.

- How to furnish a program with household objects and $25 in cash
- Ways to involve families in the child care program
- Fundraising efforts to increase resources for the family child care home
- Community resources that should be consulted regularly

Some other problem-solving techniques you might wish to try are described below.

- **Reverse brainstorming,** in which participants identify all the negative aspects of a problem that need to be remedied. This can be especially useful in examining practices to see what isn't working, such as why children are getting into fights during the day.

- The **slip method**, in which participants write their solutions to a stated problem on slips of paper that are collected and grouped into logical categories for analysis and discussion. This can be especially useful in finding plausible solutions to a specific problem, such as how to get families to pick up their children on time.

- The **Delphi technique (group approach),** in which individual participants generate as many responses to a particular problem as they can. Ideas are then consolidated and presented for the group to consider and rank in order of viability. Through this filtering process, 3 to 5 "best" solutions to particular problems can be identified.

Case Studies

The chief advantage of the case study method is that it helps participants apply what has been taught through lectures or assigned reading to meaningful examples. By providing an illustration, case studies can be a powerful tool for helping participants apply theory to their situations. Many of the vignettes and examples in the modules could be used to develop case studies.

Role-Playing

Putting oneself in another's shoes is one of the most popular training techniques. It allows participants to act out real-life situations in a risk-free environment. By seeing things from another's perspective, participants gain insight into how to approach a problem. You might consider playing roles to explore scheduling concerns, interactions with parents, or actual family child care scenarios. For example, to role-play a field trip to the library, ask providers to assume these roles:

Family child care provider	Shy toddler
Fussy infant	Children's librarian trying to enforce order
Curious toddler	Reader trying to concentrate
Chatty preschooler	Helpful parent

Through its acting, the group can identify ways to get the most from the library visit without disturbing others. Keep in mind that some adults are very uncomfortable playing roles and may prefer to watch.

Discussion Techniques: The Fishbowl, Fantasy, and Visualization

These techniques are used by trainers to stimulate discussion. In the **fishbowl** technique, participants are divided into two groups, forming an inner and an outer ring. Participants in the inner group are given an assignment based on content presented either through a lecture or reading. For example, you might ask the inner group how providers can enhance their professional image. While the inner group discusses this question aloud for 5 to 10 minutes, the outer group is asked to act as observers. At the end of the allotted time, the two groups switch roles. At the conclusion of the second discussion, both groups are asked to comment on what they've observed. Quite often, the discussion quickly becomes analytical because of mutual observations. This technique also stimulates discussion among participants who are initially shy about contributing.

Fantasy and visualization are techniques used to draw on participants' creativity. Fantasy techniques most commonly involve asking participants to reflect on "what if…" situations—for example: "What if you had unlimited financial resources. How would you equip your family child care home?" This type of exercise allows participants to think about an ideal inventory. They can then compare the ideal to reality and see where compromises are appropriate.

Fantasy can also be used to think through worst-case scenarios. For instance, you might ask participants to reflect on this scenario and discuss how they would handle the situation:

> *Suppose you firmly believe that art should reflect children's thoughts and feelings—not those of adults. Billy Z's parents let you know they are distressed because they never have any nice drawings or models to display around their home. You try talking to the Zs about your philosophy, but it seems to fall on deaf ears. When Mrs. Z makes another critical remark, you share with her an article in* Young Children *that clearly spells out your point of view: that coloring books and teacher-made models stifle children's creativity. Mrs. Z doesn't mention the article to you, so after 3 or 4 days you ask her if she or Mr. Z have any reaction to the article. She murmurs, "It was probably written by some teacher who couldn't draw and was afraid the kids would do better than she could." What should you do now?*

Visualization is a technique sometimes used by trainers to help participants relate the tasks at hand to experiences they've had in the past. For example, you might ask participants to think about an experience they've had in which they were forced to do something that made them uncomfortable. What were the circumstances? What did they do to relieve their discomfort? Did they ever get over being uncomfortable? You might use this type of reflection if you sense that participants are uncomfortable dealing with particular situations, such as having to communicate difficult information to families.

Sample Training Outline for Module 10: Guidance

Organizing training sessions in advance will help you be more effective. As you plan group sessions based on any of the modules in *Caring for Children in Family Child Care*, think about the training techniques you will use to make the experience meaningful. For example, in the outline that follows, you could use a brainstorming technique for the Discussion Questions and role-play one of the observations made by providers during Review of Activity. The following discussion questions, key points, and activities can be used for group training on Module 10. You can adapt these suggestions to meet the individual training needs of providers.

Overview

A. Opening

Begin with an open-ended question such as:

- What does "self-control" mean to you?

- How do you handle discipline at your home?

- What are some of the difficulties you experience when guiding children's behavior?

- How do you explain your discipline policy to families? What do you tell them?

B. Discussion Questions

- Why is it important for children to develop self-control?

    - To make decisions for themselves.
    - To solve their own problems.
    - To correct their mistakes.
    - To do what is expected without someone's telling them what to do.
    - To take responsibility for their own actions.
    - To learn the rules for living in our society.

- What are some of the reasons children behave inappropriately?

    - To test the limits set by adults.
    - The daily schedule doesn't meet their needs.
    - The rules at their homes are different from those at the FCC home.
    - A school or family situation is upsetting them.
    - They need attention but don't know a more acceptable way to ask for it.
    - They miss their parents.
    - They are tired, hungry, or ill.
    - They feel afraid or insecure.
    - They want to do things for themselves.

C. Review of Overview

Review the examples of strategies that providers use to guide children's behavior. Ask providers to give examples of how they use their skills in each area:

- How does your environment encourage self-control?

- What positive strategies do you use to guide children?

- How do you help children understand and express their feelings?

Discuss the vignettes and providers' responses to the questions.

- What do you think about the way the provider handled this situation?

- How would you handle a similar situation in your home?

Discuss the section on Your Own Self-Discipline.

- How does self-control affect your own behavior?

    - By guiding my behavior at work, at home, and in society.
    - By letting me respond automatically because I have learned and accepted

certain rules of behavior and want to avoid negative consequences of not following the rules.

- How does your self-control affect your work with children?

Modeling self-control helps children learn about acceptable ways to behave.

D. Ending the Session

- Answer questions and collect the pre-training assessments.

- Review the assessments. Then call providers to discuss their responses and the three to five skills and topics they want to learn more about.

Learning Activity I: Using Positive Approaches to Guide Children's Behavior

---

A. Opening

Ask providers for examples of the guidance strategies they use for children of different ages.

B. Discussion Questions

- How are "punishment" and "discipline" different?

  - Discipline means guiding and directing children in positive ways to help them learn acceptable behavior. Discipline helps children learn what they can and cannot do.
  - Punishment means controlling children through fear. It may stop children's unacceptable behavior for the moment, but doesn't help children gain internal controls.

- How can knowledge of child development help you guide children's behavior?

  - Your expectations are more realistic.
  - You can meet their changing needs.
  - Strategies that work with one age group do not necessarily work with another.

C. Review of Activity

Ask providers the ages of the children in their care. Focus your discussion on the ages with the highest representation, but be sure to spend some time on each age group. Encourage providers to give examples from their own experiences, as noted on the charts they completed in the learning activity. When appropriate, offer examples from your own observations in FCC homes of how providers guide the behavior of a multi-age group. Responses such as the following are appropriate:

- What can you do to guide **infants'** behavior?

  - Organize routines so infants don't have to wait.
  - Arrange the home so infants can explore safely.
  - Remove hazards and inappropriate temptations.
  - Keep infants away from potential problems.

- Respond to crying immediately.
- Offer infants an alternative toy or object.
- Separate infants who are hurting each other.
- Use tone of voice, facial expressions, gestures, and speech to express feelings.
- Give infants a chance to work things out themselves, if the situation is safe.
- Use "no" sparingly.

- What can you do to guide **toddlers'** behavior?

  - Give simple, clear choices.
  - Use positive suggestions.
  - Redirect to an acceptable alternative.
  - Provide games and other opportunities to say "no."
  - Let them know you recognize their feelings.
  - Say you will not allow them to hurt people or things.

- What can you do to guide **preschoolers'** behavior?

  - Provide a schedule that provides order, consistency, and flexibility.
  - Reinforce positive behavior.
  - Suggest physically active activities when children seem restless.
  - Involve children in making rules.
  - Set up a system for taking turns with popular items.
  - Invite children to help with meaningful tasks.
  - Hold an out-of-control child until he or she gains control again.

- What can you do to guide **school-age children's** behavior?

  - Listen and help children solve their own problems.
  - Pay attention to school-age children, especially when they arrive.
  - Provide a quiet place where children can do homework if they choose.
  - Ask about and respond to children's interests.
  - Allow children to select, plan, and carry out their activities.
  - Provide a safe storage space for belongings and projects.
  - Encourage older children to be involved with the younger ones.

D. Additional Resources/Activities

Set out poster board and markers. Ask providers to identify the suggestions in the learning activity that were the most helpful to them in guiding children's behavior. Invite them to make signs for their home to remind them of those suggestions.

E. Ending the Session

- Collect completed charts from this activity. You can review them later, discuss during phone conferences if needed, and return to providers at the next meeting.

- Give a brief overview of the next learning activity.

- Ask providers to draw plans of their indoor and outdoor environments, label features that promote children's self-control, and bring the plans to the next meeting. If possible, providers should also bring photographs showing how they have set up their homes and outdoor areas.

Learning Activity II: Arranging Your Home to Promote Self-Control

A. Opening

Ask providers to share the plans and photographs of their environments and discuss how different features promote self-discipline. Address the following points:

- Identifying which areas of the home are off-limits to children.

- Designating areas for different kinds of activities.

- Establishing comfortable places for quiet activities.

- Setting aside a place for older children to play and store their materials.

- Allowing for traffic flow.

B. Discussion Questions

- How can you arrange the environment so it encourages self-control?

  - Keep unsafe items out of reach.
  - Provide duplicates of favorite items.
  - Store materials on low, open shelves where children can reach them.
  - Use picture and word labels to show where things go.
  - Arrange the furniture to encourage appropriate behavior.
  - Allow for traffic flow.

- What do children learn from a well-organized environment?

  - Where they are allowed to play.
  - To respect the rights of others.
  - That their belongings will be safe.
  - To find the toys and materials they want to use.
  - To put things away when they are finished.
  - To care for toys and other materials.

C. Review of Activity

- Ask providers to share their responses to the chart, Arranging Your Home to Promote Self-Control, and compare them to those provided at the end of the module.

- Discuss problem behaviors encountered by providers and how rearranging the environment might eliminate them.

- Encourage providers to help each other develop solutions.

D. Additional Resources/Activities

- Bring illustrations that show how furniture and materials can be arranged to promote self-control.

- Arrange for providers to visit each other's homes and share ideas.

E. Ending the Session

- Collect completed charts from this activity. You can review them later, discuss during phone conferences if needed, and return to providers at the next meeting.

- Give a brief overview of the next learning activity.

- Ask if providers have (or have access to) tape players. Suggest that they tape themselves as they interact with children.

Learning Activity III: Using Language to Provide Positive Guidance

A. Opening

Begin this session by having providers think about when they were very young.

- How did the words and tone of voice used by adults affect you?

- How did you feel when an adult yelled or used harsh words? How did you feel when an adult spoke quietly, using a firm tone of voice?

B. Discussion Questions

- What are some guidelines for using language to guide children's behavior?

  - Use a quiet but firm tone of voice so children feel safe and cared for.
  - Get close enough to children so they can hear a normal voice. This avoids shouting and startling children.
  - Crouch or kneel at the child's level so you can have a private discussion.
  - Look into the child's eyes, touch an arm or shoulder, and give full attention.
  - Offer choices only when you mean them.
  - Give directions in a positive way.
  - Do not compare one child to another.

- How can you use clear statements to explain to children what they may and may not do? (Ask providers for examples.)

  - Describe what happened in the situation to which you are responding.
  - Tell the child what behavior is not acceptable.
  - Tell the child what behavior is acceptable.
  - Explain a consequence for the behavior.

C. Review of Activity

Have providers work with one or two others to share their responses to the situations in the learning activity.

- How similar are the responses?
- In what ways are they different?

Ask each team to present what they learned from one another. Discuss any questions or areas of disagreement that came up.

D. Additional Resources/Activities

- If providers brought tape recordings of their conversations with children, invite them to share them with the group. Lead a discussion, pointing out positive interactions you heard.

- Describe example situations where providers would need to step in and use language to guide children's behavior. Have the group identify more situations.

E. Ending the Session

- Collect completed charts from this activity. You can review them later, discuss during phone conferences if needed, and return to providers at the next meeting.

- Give a brief overview of the next learning activity.

Learning Activity IV: Setting Rules and Limits

A. Opening

Ask each provider to share one rule they have for their FCC home. Make a list on a flip chart. Then ask:

- Why do you need these rules?

- How do you know when a rule is or is not working?

- How frequently are they updated?

- How are children involved in setting rules?

- How do you help children understand the reasons for the rules?

B. Discussion Questions

- Why is it important for FCC homes to have rules and limits?

    - When they know adults have set limits, children feel safe and free to explore.
    - Rules and limits help adults and children understand what behaviors are acceptable.

- Why is it important to have just enough rules?

    - When there are too many rules, children can't remember them.
    - When there are too few, the environment might be unsafe or disorderly.

- Why might you need to have different rules for different ages?

    - Rules should correspond to children's stages of development.
    - Rules should be changed as children grow and develop.

C. Review of Activity

- Have providers practice stating rules positively so that they remind children of what to do.

- Ask volunteers to share the rules they have established in their homes and their responses to the questions in Learning Activity IV. Stress the importance of making sure rules fit the needs of individual children.

D. Additional Resources/Activities

Set out poster board and markers so providers can make signs to hang in their homes. Explain that the signs will help them remember to make positive statements that tell children what to do, rather than what not to do.

E. Ending the Session

- Collect completed charts from this activity. You can review them later, discuss during phone conferences if needed, and return to providers at the next meeting.

- Give a brief overview of the next learning activity and the Summarizing Your Progress section at the end of the module.

Learning Activity V: Responding to Problem Behaviors and Summarizing Your Progress

---

A. Opening

Ask providers:

- Why do we use the term "problem behavior" instead of "bad behavior" or "problem child"?

- How do you handle biting, kicking, temper tantrums, and so on?

- Have you tried any of the suggestions in the learning activity?

B. Discussion Questions

- How would you respond to the children in the examples on the first page of this learning activity? How would your response help the child develop and learn?

- What problem behaviors have you had to handle? What were the children trying to express through their behavior? How did you respond to each child? Stress the following points:

    - Often young children cannot express their feelings verbally.
    - Sometimes children don't know why they are feeling the way they do. They need an adult to help them figure out what they are feeling and why.
    - It's okay for children to have negative feelings.
    - Adults can help children learn to express their negative feelings without hurting anyone.
    - Some children feel better when they can release their feelings—throwing beanbags, hammering. Other children respond better to quiet activities.
    - Some behaviors that require adult patience are typical of particular developmental stages.

C. Review of Activity

Ask for volunteers to discuss the child on whom they focused in the learning activity and the plan they developed with the family to address the problem behavior. To maintain confidentiality, providers should not use the child's name. Stress the process used to find out what was causing the child's behavior.

D. Summarizing Your Progress

- Ask providers to share one item from their summary of what they learned while working on this module.

- Ask providers to share some of the ways they adapted or changed their discipline policies and how the revisions were shared with families. How have families responded to the revised policies?

E. Ending the Session

- Collect provider's charts and respond to the progress summaries and discipline policies. Review and discuss these during phone conferences.

- Set up times to visit homes to administer knowledge and competency assessments.

If you are planning group training sessions using the modules in *Caring for Children in Family Child Care*, you may find it helpful to use the Form for Planning Group Sessions in Appendix A.

III. One-on-One Training/Mentoring

III. One-on-One Training/Mentoring

This chapter explains how a trainer or mentor might work with providers on-site (at the family child care home) to complete *Caring for Children in Family Child Care* as a self-paced training course. Such an approach should be based on the adult learning principles outlined in the previous chapter. To facilitate this process, you will find charts that summarize what providers and trainers/mentors do during each module, suggestions on how to give feedback to providers, and strategies for extending learning.

Completing the Introduction

Caring for Children in Family Child Care begins with two important initial steps: an overall self-assessment and development of an individual training plan.

Overall Self-Assessment

After reading the Introduction, and before beginning the training modules, providers assess their skills by ranking how frequently they carry out basic activities identified for each module. This is not a test; it is an exercise designed to give providers an overview of the program and help them decide which modules they will work on first. You may want to acknowledge that it can be difficult for providers to identify which skills they need to develop further and what areas they want to know more about. Encourage providers to complete the self-assessment as honestly as possible. Honest answers will allow them to develop training plans that reflect their needs and interests.

Individual Training Plan

When a provider first enters the program, it is helpful if you can schedule a one-hour observation of the provider working with children. If a provider seems uncomfortable with the observation process, explain that observation is an important training tool. Observations are used throughout the training program to provide feedback to providers on their progress in applying the information and skills they develop as they work on each module.

During a home visit, discuss your observation notes and the self-assessment results, then work with the provider to develop an individual training plan. This plan should reflect the provider's skill level. The provider then selects, with your help, the first modules to work on. If you are working with several providers, you may want to adjust individual plans so that several providers are working on the same module at the same time. Coordinating training plans in this way will allow you to conduct group meetings where providers can learn from and provide support to each other. (Strategies for conducting group training were addressed in Chapter II of this Guide.)

Working Through a Module

Although the content and activities in the modules vary substantially, providers follow the same process for completing each one. It can take four to six weeks to complete all the learning activities in each module. The entire training program involves a commitment of 12 to 18 months. Each of the sections of a module are described below.

The Overview

The overview introduces and defines the topic addressed in the module. It explains why the topic is important and gives concrete examples of how providers demonstrate their competence in that functional area. Providers read three short vignettes and answer questions to help them think about the topic. The last activity in the overview is an opportunity to consider the topic in relation to a provider's own experiences.

The Pre-Training Assessment

The pre-training assessment is a list of key provider strategies in each functional area. Providers indicate whether they do these things regularly, sometimes, or not enough, and identify three to five skills they wish to improve or topics they wish to learn more about.

After completing the overview and the pre-training assessment, providers discuss their responses with their trainer during a home visit or phone conference. They then begin the learning activities for the module.

Learning Activities

Each module has four to six learning activities. The activities begin with objectives—statements of what providers will learn—and several pages of information about the topic. After reading about the topic, providers apply the information as they care for children. This might involve responding to questions, trying suggestions from the reading, planning and implementing an activity, or completing written observations of children. Providers might want to use some of their responses to learning activities for their CDA Professional Resource File. After completing each learning activity, providers discuss the skills and topics with their trainer during a home visit, phone conference, and/or provider group training. The group trainings are opportunities to discuss progress, ask questions, and provide and receive feedback from peers.

Summarizing Your Progress

After completing all the learning activities in a module, providers review their responses to the pre-training assessment and write a brief summary of what they have learned and the skills they have acquired. They then discuss any remaining questions with their trainer/mentor and decide if they are ready for the module assessment process.

The Assessment Process

Caring for Children in Family Child Care includes two kinds of assessments for each module: a knowledge assessment and a competency assessment. (The assessments and instructions for using them are in Chapter IV.)

The *knowledge assessment* is a paper-and-pencil exercise that tests the provider's knowledge of the concepts presented in the module. The test can be given during an assessment home visit. In order to pass, a provider must achieve a score of at least 80 percent. If a provider does not achieve this score, you should note which answers were wrong and suggest reviewing or repeating the relevant learning activity before retaking the test.

The *competency assessment* is a one-hour observation of the provider working with children. Trainers/mentors use a module-specific list of indicators to assess the provider's demonstrated skills. Your role includes observing the provider working with children, determining whether the criteria for successful completion were met, and discussing the results of your observation with the provider. You can assess a provider's competence in two to three areas at a time (for example, Self, Social, and Guidance). If a provider has successfully completed the assessments, you can discuss starting the next module. If the provider needs to spend more time on the module, you might suggest repeating some of the learning activities to acquire the needed skills or offer additional resources and opportunities to acquire the additional skills and knowledge.

Documentation of Progress

When providers have successfully completed the module assessments, they can record their progress on the Individual Tracking Form (included in Appendix D). Trainers who are responsible for overseeing staff development for a group of providers may want to use the Group Tracking Form (also in Appendix D). In addition, it is critically important for providers to formally document all contact hours by subject area. For this purpose, we have developed a form for the Documentation of Training Hours, which can be found in Appendix E.

Offering Feedback Through Phone Conferences and Home Visits

Feedback to providers takes place many times during the training and is crucial to the success of the *Caring for Children in Family Child Care* training program. Regular contact with providers, ideally at least once a week, is particularly important when this training is used as a self-instructional program. If possible, try to schedule at least two home visits and conduct several phone conferences for each module. Modules with more learning activities will take more time to complete.

Phone conferences may be as short as 15 minutes or may take longer, depending on how much feedback and support are needed. Home visits will generally last longer. They are recommended at the beginning of the program when the provider and trainer/mentor develop the individual training plan, and whenever a learning activity is best discussed in person rather than on the phone.

Both home visits and phone conferences can give you the opportunity to:

- answer providers' questions;
- offer support in preparing to do learning activities;
- make suggestions and hear concerns about progress;
- recognize and reinforce new skills and knowledge;
- provide resources; and
- help providers repeat activities they may have misunderstood the first time.

It is best to provide feedback for the overview and pre-training assessment, and for *each* learning activity before the provider goes on to the next one. You want to be sure that the provider has understood the content, and the best time to do this is while the responses are still fresh in the provider's mind. A full understanding of each activity is particularly important in modules where one learning activity builds on the results of the previous one.

The feedback schedule that follows summarizes for each module when home visits and phone conferences are recommended.

Module Feedback Schedule

Module	Home Visit	Phone Conference	Phone Conf./ Home Visit
1. Safe	-Learning Activity III -Assessment	-Learning Activities I, II, IV, & V -Summarizing Your Progress	-Overview & Pre-training Assessment -Learning Activity VI
2. Healthy	-Learning Activity III -Assessment	-Summarizing Your Progress	-Overview & Pre-training Assessment -Learning Activities I, II, IV, & V
3. Learning Environment	-Learning Activity III -Assessment	-Learning Activity IV -Summarizing Your Progress	-Overview & Pre-training Assessment -Learning Activities I & II
4. Physical	-Assessment	-Summarizing Your Progress	-Overview & Pre-training Assessment -Learning Activities I, II, III, IV, & V
5. Cognitive	-Learning Activity III -Assessment	-Learning Activities I & V -Summarizing Your Progress	-Overview & Pre-training Assessment -Learning Activities II & IV
6. Communication	-Learning Activity II -Assessment	-Learning Activity I -Summarizing Your Progress	-Overview & Pre-training Assessment -Learning Activities III, IV, & V
7. Creative	-Learning Activity I -Assessment	-Summarizing Your Progress	-Overview & Pre-training Assessment -Learning Activities II, III, & IV

Module Feedback Schedule (continued)

Module	Home Visit	Phone Conference	Phone Conf./ Home Visit
8. Self	-Learning Activity IV -Assessment	-Learning Activity I -Summarizing Your Progress	-Overview & Pre-training Assessment -Learning Activities II, III, V, & VI
9. Social	-Learning Activity II -Assessment	-Summarizing Your Progress	-Overview & Pre-training Assessment -Learning Activities I, III, IV, & V
10. Guidance	-Learning Activities II & V -Assessments	-Summarizing Your Progress	-Overview & Pre-training Assessment -Learning Activities I, III, & IV
11. Families	-Learning Activity VI -Assessments	-Learning Activity III -Summarizing Your Progress	-Overview & Pre-training Assessment -Learning Activities I, II, IV, & V
12. Program Management	-Learning Activities II & III -Assessments	-Learning Activity IV -Summarizing Your Progress	-Overview & Pre-training Assessment -Learning Activity III
13. Professionalism	-Learning Activity III -Assessments	-Learning Activities I & II -Summarizing Your Progress	-Overview & Pre-training Assessment -Learning Activity IV & V

Suggestions for Providing Feedback

Listed below are some suggestions for providing feedback during phone conferences or home visits. You can adapt these suggestions to meet your own style of training and what you know about each provider.

- **Review the provider's responses in each learning activity ahead of time to prepare for the conference.** This is especially important when you need to give feedback on inappropriate responses. Consider carefully how to approach the session so that your comments are constructive and do not discourage a provider from trying the activity again.

- **Begin with an open-ended question**, such as "How did you feel about this activity?" or "Were you surprised by anything you read?". Take a few minutes to discuss each provider's responses to your questions.

- **Ask questions to determine the level of difficulty**, such as:
  "Were some parts of the activity easier than others?"
  "Were there any problem areas for you?"
  "Was anything unclear or confusing?"

- **Acknowledge accurate, appropriate responses.** For example: "You phrased that well. You told him clearly what you expected, but you were careful to show him you understood his feelings."

- **Relate the provider's responses to information in the text:** "You clearly understood what is discussed in the section on challenging behaviors."

- **Ask questions about inappropriate responses.** Rather than simply correcting these responses, help the provider think about why a response is inappropriate and what affect it might have on a child. For example:
  "What are the reasons for Jan's behavior?"
  "What do you want the children to learn from this activity?"
  "What message would this statement give to the child?"

- **Help the provider arrive at an appropriate response.** You might say:
  "Let's look back at the text to see if there's another way to phrase this so that it still accomplishes your goals but doesn't make the child feel badly."

The underlying goal of providing feedback is to improve a provider's skills and knowledge. If you think the provider has not understood the information presented in the module, use the feedback conference to review and explain the information, and the strategies for extending learning (included with the charts presented in the next section) to help providers develop competence.

Encouraging Experienced Providers to Serve as Mentors

Many organizations that offer training for FCC providers have established a system for using experienced, skilled providers as mentors who offer feedback to individuals working on the modules. Mentors, who may be identified through their participation in group trainings, often establish relationships with other providers that continue beyond the training program. Once this training program has been in place for a year or more, current providers will have completed their training and only new providers will be working on the modules. At this point a system of provider mentors can be very useful in supporting new providers and encouraging them as they progress through the training modules.

Try to arrange subsidies to pay for substitute care in the FCC homes of providers who are serving as mentors. This will allow the mentors to make home visits, conduct observations, and provide feedback on specific learning activities.

What Providers and Trainers/Mentors Do in Each Module

The following charts summarize what the provider and trainer/mentor does in each section of the 13 modules. Individual providers, trainers and mentors have different learning and interaction styles. Thus, these charts do not present hard-and-fast rules to be followed inflexibly. Rather, they summarize what providers are asked to do in each learning activity and suggest constructive ways for trainers or mentors to offer support. Each chart is followed by suggested strategies that can be used with individual providers or during group training for extending learning.

Completing Module 1: Safe

LEARNING ACTIVITY	WHAT PROVIDER DOES	WHAT TRAINER/MENTOR DOES

Overview and Pre-Training Assessment	Read about safety and provider competence.
	
	Write brief responses to situational safety questions.
	
	Answer questions about personal safety experiences.
	
	Complete pre-training assessment and list three to five skills to improve or topics to learn more about.
		Review the ongoing written observations of provider.
		
		Discuss during a **phone conference** or **home visit** provider's:
		
		    responses to situational questions;
		
		    personal safety experiences and how they relate to keeping children safe; and
		
		    pre-training assessment.
		
		Validate where possible with written observations.

I. Creating and Maintaining a Safe Environment	Read about safety precautions and rules for maintaining a safe environment. Use safety checklists to evaluate conditions in the indoor and outdoor environment. List items that are unsafe and what needs to be done to improve the safety of the environment.	During a **phone conference** discuss the checklists and potential dangers the provider identified. Help provider plan for making the needed changes.
II. Ensuring the Safety of Toys and Equipment	Read about how to assess the safety of toys and materials. Use a checklist to assess the safety of two toys and several pieces of equipment in the FCC home.	During a **phone conference**, discuss any toys or equipment that provider thinks are unsafe and what repairs are needed to make them safe. Suggest that provider schedule a time to check the safety of toys and equipment regularly.

Module 1: Safe (Continued)

LEARNING ACTIVITY	WHAT PROVIDER DOES	WHAT TRAINER/MENTOR DOES
III. Meeting the Safety Needs of Each Child	Read about precautions that correspond to children's ages and developmental stages. Conduct several observations of one child during a one week period. Describe what the child did, safety hazards identified, and what to do to keep children safe.	During a **home visit**, discuss and review child development and safe caregiving practices with provider. Review and discuss the safety observations and help provider implement needed changes.
IV. Responding in Emergencies	Read about developing contingency plans, evacuation procedures, using fire extinguishers, responding to children's emergencies, and providing first aid. Review own contingency and evacuation plans and answer questions about how these plans are used during an emergency. Answer questions about how to respond in different emergency situations.	During a **phone conference**, discuss provider's answers to the questions and discuss any items that need clarification. Encourage provider to practice emergency procedures on a regular basis. Provide additional resources and training if provider needs to learn more about this topic.
V. Ensuring Children's Safety Away From the FCC Home	Read about preparing for neighborhood walks, transporting children by car, walking safely near traffic, and planning safe field trips. Record the FCC home's rules and procedures for ensuring children's safety on field trips; identify additional safety precautions to ensure children's safety.	During a **phone conference**, discuss provider's answers to questions on FCC home rules and procedures. Help provider implement additional safety precautions.

Module 1: Safe (Continued)

LEARNING ACTIVITY	WHAT PROVIDER DOES	WHAT TRAINER/MENTOR DOES
VI. Helping Children Learn to Keep Themselves Safe	Read about ways to help children learn to keep themselves safe. Work with the children to develop safety limits for one activity or area of the home. Answer questions about this process and the limits developed.	During a **phone conference** or **home visit**, discuss provider's responses to the questions. If possible, observe provider communicating safety rules to children. Discuss the need for other safety rules based on materials and equipment in the environment and the developmental stages of the children.
Summarizing Your Progress	Review responses to pre-training assessment and summarize knowledge and skills acquired in completing this module.	During a **phone conference** discuss provider's responses; then schedule a **home visit** to complete the assessment for this module. The competency assessment should include observation of a fire drill.

Strategies for Extending Learning

- Have providers lie or kneel on the floor to view the environment from the perspective of a child and then discuss the experience, noting potential hazards that they discovered.

- Distribute information about safety training courses such as Red Cross workshops; encourage providers to attend.

- Visit the Web sites of the American Academy of Pediatrics and the Consumer Product Safety Commission for information on keeping children safe. Suggest ways to share the information with families.

- Brainstorm with providers ways to individualize the safety checklist to reflect the layout, furnishings, materials, and equipment in their FCC homes.

- Ask a fireman or other expert to provide training on how to respond during emergencies and natural disasters such as hurricanes, floods, and tornadoes.

- Put together an FCC scrapbook highlighting strategies providers have used to keep children safe in emergencies or crisis situations.

Completing Module 2: Healthy

LEARNING ACTIVITY	WHAT PROVIDER DOES	WHAT TRAINER/MENTOR DOES

Overview and Pre-Training Assessment	Read about helping children develop good health and hygiene habits; learning to recognize signs of possible child abuse and neglect.
	
	Write brief responses to situational health questions.
	
	Answer questions about personal health and nutrition.
	
	Complete pre-training assessment and list three to five skills to improve or topics to learn more about.
		Review the ongoing written observations of provider.
		
		Discuss during a **phone conference** or **home visit** provider's:
		
		    responses to situational questions;
		
		    personal health habits and how they relate to keeping children healthy; and
		
		    pre-training assessment.
		
		Validate where possible with written observations.

I. Maintaining an Environment That Promotes Wellness	Read about maintaining a hygienic environment: using bleach solutions for sanitation, diapering and hand washing procedures, caring for children who are ill, contagious diseases, administering medication, HIV/AIDS. Use a health checklist to assess the environment. List items that need improvement and plans for making changes. Make needed changes to make the environment more hygienic.	During a **phone conference** or **home visit**, discuss provider's completed checklist. Review items needing improvement and changes that provider wants to make. Guide provider to add other items that could be improved.

Module 2: Healthy (Continued)

LEARNING ACTIVITY	WHAT PROVIDER DOES	WHAT TRAINER/MENTOR DOES
II. Helping Children Develop Good Health Habits	Read about modeling good health practices and using daily activities and routines for health education. Plan and conduct a health education activity. Answer questions about what happened during the activity and what might be done differently if it were repeated.	During a **phone conference** or **home visit**, discuss the health education activity and provider's answers to the questions. Help provider recognize how daily routines help children develop good health habits. Collect and share materials the provider can use to plan health education activities.
III. Helping Children Develop Good Nutrition Habits	Read about nutrition education, feeding infants, eating family-style, and cooking with children. Answer questions about different ways adults feed infants. Plan and conduct a cooking activity, answer questions about what happened during the activity and what should be done differently next time.	During a **home visit**, review answers to questions on feeding infants. If provider cares for infants, discuss what provider does to make feeding time relaxing and pleasant and, if applicable, what changes should be made. Offer to assist in collecting resources and ingredients for the cooking activity. If possible, observe provider implementing the cooking activity. Discuss provider's written responses to the questions and help provider plan ways to involve children in cooking food for meals and snacks.

Module 2: Healthy (Continued)

LEARNING ACTIVITY	WHAT PROVIDER DOES	WHAT TRAINER/MENTOR DOES
IV. Recognizing Child Abuse and Neglect	Read the definitions of different kinds of child abuse and neglect and the signs of physical abuse, neglect, sexual abuse, and emotional abuse. Also read about how to recognize child abuse and neglect through conversations and interviews. Select two children who show emotions in different ways. Observe the two children for two to three days and keep notes on how the children show that they are happy, sad, or afraid. Use the observation notes to answer questions about the two children.	During a **phone conference** or **home visit**, discuss written observations of two children and help provider recognize how each child is unique. Ensure that provider understands signs of possible child abuse and neglect. Ensure that provider knows how child abuse and neglect are defined in her state.
V. Reporting Suspected Cases of Child Abuse and Neglect	Read about what providers must do to report suspected cases of child abuse and neglect. Complete a chart summarizing the FCC program's policy on reporting child abuse and neglect. Review a checklist of what providers should do when getting ready to file a report. Read about how to overcome barriers to reporting. Answer questions about a provider's responsibilities for reporting child abuse and neglect.	During a **phone conference** or **home visit**, ensure that provider has a copy of the FCC program's policy and procedures for reporting child abuse and neglect. Ensure that provider understands the requirement to report suspected child abuse or neglect. Review answers to the questions and help provider compare them to those provided at the end of the module. Answer provider's additional questions and help alleviate any remaining concerns regarding reporting suspected cases of child abuse and neglect.

Module 2: Healthy (Continued)

LEARNING ACTIVITY	WHAT PROVIDER DOES	WHAT TRAINER/MENTOR DOES
Summarizing Your Progress	Review responses to pre-training assessment and summarize knowledge and skills acquired in completing this module.	During a **phone conference** discuss provider's responses; then schedule a **home visit** to complete the assessment for this module.

Strategies for Extending Learning

- Have providers review and discuss their menus and recommend changes, if necessary, to ensure that foods served to children meet USDA guidelines and that they are high in nutrients and low in fats, salt, and sugar. Share USDA cycle menus to give guidance in planning meals.

- Suggest that families ask parents to share their favorite recipes. Provide the materials providers will need to make picture recipe cards.

- Encourage providers to have children plant a vegetable garden. Once the produce is ripe, children can pick fresh vegetables for snacks and meals.

- Keep and share your file of recipes and plans for providers to use for simple cooking activities.

- Ask providers to review their procedures for conducting routines such as hand washing, disinfecting toys and equipment, diapering, and serving meals. Provide materials for making charts that summarize these procedures and that can be hung in appropriate areas of the home. The charts could be illustrated with photographs of children and providers performing these routines.

- Encourage providers to contact their local government's Child Protective Services or child abuse hotline to receive literature on child abuse and neglect and to learn about workshops or seminars given locally.

Completing Module 3: Learning Environment

LEARNING ACTIVITY	WHAT PROVIDER DOES	WHAT TRAINER/MENTOR DOES
Overview and Pre-Training Assessment	Read about the outdoor and indoor learning environments and about provider competence. Write brief responses to situational questions about creating and using an environment. Answer questions about being personally affected by different environments. Complete pre-training assessment and list three to five skills to improve or topics to learn more about.	Review the ongoing written observations of provider and the learning environment. Discuss during a **phone conference** or **home visit** provider's: responses to situational questions; personal experiences with physical environments and how they relate to creating a supportive environment for children; and pre-training assessment. Validate where possible with written observations.
I. Using Your Home as a Learning Environment	Read about selecting appropriate furnishings and materials, review lists of suggested toys and materials for children of different ages, read about establishing activity areas, and consider storage options. Complete an inventory of materials and equipment in the FCC home. List materials to add, how to obtain or make them, and how to display them.	During a **phone conference** or **home visit**, discuss provider's inventory and whether it meets the needs and interests of the children. Help provider access a local FCC Resource Library. Provide resources on using recycled items to make toys that are open-ended and appropriate for a wide age range.

Module 3: Learning Environment (Continued)

LEARNING ACTIVITY	WHAT PROVIDER DOES	WHAT TRAINER/MENTOR DOES
II. Shaping the Messages in Your Learning Environment	Read about the messages children receive from the arrangement of the environment. Complete a chart identifying messages in the environment and new ideas to try. Discuss ideas with trainer and agree on changes to make.	During a **phone conference** or **home visit**, discuss provider's chart of messages in the environment and new ideas to try. Offer suggestions about how the provider can obtain the materials needed to make changes. Encourage provider to observe children to see how they react to the changes.
III. Using the Outdoors as a Learning Environment	Read about how to create an outdoor environment that allows children to use and develop their senses and their fine and gross motor skills. Draw a picture of the outdoor area and label where different activities take place. Make a list of equipment and materials children can use outdoors. Plan additions and improvements.	During a **home visit** review provider's drawing of the outdoor area. Discuss the desired changes and how they will improve the outdoor learning environment. Provide information about the local FCC Resource Library. Discuss how the provider will implement the changes.

Module 3: Learning Environment (Continued)

LEARNING ACTIVITY	WHAT PROVIDER DOES	WHAT TRAINER/MENTOR DOES
IV. Managing the Day	Read about developing a daily plan to meet the needs of children. Review a sample daily plan for family child care. Read about the importance of routines as times for learning. Select two to three daily routines and describe the problems encountered and possible solutions. Write down the daily schedule for the FCC home and use a checklist to assess how appropriate it is. Rewrite the daily plan, making any necessary changes.	During a **phone conference** reinforce the concept of daily routines as opportunities for a variety of learning experiences. Review the daily plan that provider follows, and discuss how it is working and if any changes are needed. Assist provider in revising the plan if necessary. During the next observation, help provider learn to adapt the daily plan when necessary and to take advantage of "teachable moments."
Summarizing Your Progress	Review responses to pre-training assessment and summarize knowledge and skills acquired in completing this module.	During a **phone conference** discuss provider's responses; then schedule a **home visit** to complete the assessment for this module.

Strategies for Extending Learning

- Identify indoor activities that can also take place outdoors. Discuss questions such as these: "What do you need to do to take this activity outdoors?" "How would the experience be different for the children?" "What indoor activities can't take place outdoors?" Ask providers to plan and implement some of their suggestions.

- Ask providers to draw an ideal way to arrange their indoor or outdoor (or both) environments. Discuss why the new plan meets the needs of the children better than the current environment. Help providers use their plans to create improve their environments.

- Assist providers in collecting a variety of materials (e.g., dramatic play props, cardboard boxes, plastic containers, computer paper, fabric scraps). Help providers store and display these so children can select what they want to use and put things away when they are done. Suggest that providers take pictures of the children using the items.

Module 3: Learning Environment (Continued)

- Observe a transition that the provider has found to be problematic. Share your observation notes and help plan a different approach for handling the transition.

- Suggest that providers work together to assess each other's environments (perhaps using an instrument such as the Family Day Care Rating Scale [FDCRS]). Providers can work together to review the assessments and develop strategies for improving the environment.

- Have providers describe strategies they use to create a learning environment in their home without losing their homey atmosphere. During home visits, take photographs depicting use of the strategies. Use the photos and written descriptions to create several copies of a notebook that can be included in the FCC Resource Library.

Completing Module 4: Physical

LEARNING ACTIVITY	WHAT PROVIDER DOES	WHAT TRAINER/MENTOR DOES
Overview and Pre-Training Assessment	Read about gross and fine motor development and discuss provider competence. Write brief responses to situational questions about promoting physical development. Answer questions about taking care of own body. Complete pre-training assessment and list three to five skills to improve or topics to learn more about.	Review the written observations of provider. Discuss during a **phone conference** or **home visit**, provider's: responses to situational questions; plans to improve posture and movements so that provider is physically able to care for children; and pre-training assessment. Validate where possible with written observations.
I. Promoting Physical Development Throughout the Day	Read about the typical pattern of physical development and how to promote physical skills through interactions with children and during daily routines such as dressing, grooming, toileting, and eating. Observe and take notes on two children over a two-day period. Describe differences in each child's fine and gross motor skills and how physical development was supported.	During a **phone conference** or **home visit**, discuss provider's observation notes and answers to questions. Help provider identify the differences in the two children's physical development. Discuss how to apply the information learned in this learning activity to support children's physical development.

Module 4: Physical (Continued)

LEARNING ACTIVITY	WHAT PROVIDER DOES	WHAT TRAINER/MENTOR DOES
II. Observing and Planning for Gross Motor Development	Read about how children of different ages develop gross motor skills and how providers can promote development by taking children outdoors for active play and through music and movement activities. Plan and implement an open-ended, multi-age activity to promote children's gross motor skills. Answer questions about what took place during the activity.	During a **phone conference** or **home visit**, ask provider to explain why the activity was open-ended and how children of different ages were involved. If possible, observe provider and children during gross motor activity. Encourage provider to include outdoor play in the schedule every day.
III. Observing and Planning for Fine Motor Development	Read about how children of different ages develop fine motor skills and the provider's role in facilitating this development. Plan and implement an open-ended, multi-age activity to promote children's fine motor development. Answer questions about what took place during the activity.	During a **phone conference** or **home visit**, ask provider to explain why the activity was open-ended and how children of different ages were involved. If possible, observe provider and children during fine motor activity. Discuss with the provider how children develop fine motor skills through play and during routines.
IV. Creating an Environment That Promotes Physical Development	Review and add to a chart showing how different activities provide opportunities for fine and gross motor play. Identify for each child in care, a fine or gross motor skill that the child is working on. List toys and materials in the FCC home, or that could be provided, that will promote development of the physical skill.	During a **phone conference** or **home visit**, discuss the provider's completed chart and how the toys and materials listed will help the child develop the specific physical skill. Suggest other activities and routines that might help the children develop the noted physical skills.

Module 4: Physical (Continued)

LEARNING ACTIVITY	WHAT PROVIDER DOES	WHAT TRAINER/MENTOR DOES
V. Helping Children Develop a Sense of Self Through Physical Development	Read about how physical development is an important factor in social and emotional development and what providers can do to encourage a positive sense of self. List physical activities and materials that can help children develop a positive sense of self. Record ways of interacting with children to promote physical development.	During a **phone conference** or **home visit**, discuss provider's responses and give suggestions if needed. Discuss individual children with provider and develop ideas together. If possible, observe the program and offer feedback on the ways provider supports the development of strong self-concepts.
Summarizing Your Progress	Review responses to pre-training assessment and summarize knowledge and skills acquired in completing this module.	During a **phone conference** discuss provider's responses; then schedule a **home visit** to complete the assessment for this module.

Strategies for Extending Learning

- Work with a group of providers to develop checklists for gross and fine motor skills for the FCC program. You might want to use a published assessment tool such as the Early Learning Accomplishment Profile for Younger Children (E-LAP) or the Learning Accomplishment Profile (LAP) from the Chapel Hill Training Outreach Project as a starting point. Encourage providers to use the checklists as a part of their observation and recording systems.

- Use the information in the module to make a large chart showing the stages of children's physical development. Post the chart in the workshop room, and ask providers to brainstorm how they might use the information to help children gain physical skills. Discuss the suggested provider practices.

- Plan and conduct a "messy activities" workshop in which providers play as children would. Include activities such as finger painting, water play, food preparation, and playing with dough. Discuss the small muscle skills that children develop through these activities.

- Observe any children whom providers are concerned about—children who seem to have unusual delays in fine or gross motor skill development. Discuss your observations with the providers, and, if needed, with the children's families. Encourage families to arrange for professional follow-up if necessary.

Completing Module 5: Cognitive

LEARNING ACTIVITY	WHAT PROVIDER DOES	WHAT TRAINER/MENTOR DOES
Overview and Pre-Training Assessment	Read about cognitive development and provider competence. Write brief responses to situational questions about promoting children's cognitive development. List factors that have helped you be a successful learner. Complete pre-training assessment and list three to five skills to improve or topics to learn more about.	Review the ongoing written observations of provider. Discuss during a **phone conference** or **home visit**, provider's: responses to situational questions; understanding of theories about cognitive development and how they relate to helping children become lifelong learners; and pre-training assessment. Validate where possible with written observations.
I. Using Your Knowledge of Child Development to Promote Cognitive Development	Read about the cognitive development of infants, toddlers, preschoolers, and school-age children. Write examples of how providers can promote children's cognitive development.	During a **phone conference** discuss the provider's examples. Point out other ways provider has demonstrated skills in promoting cognitive development. Encourage provider to add to the chart while completing the remaining learning activities.

Module 5: Cognitive (Continued)

LEARNING ACTIVITY	WHAT PROVIDER DOES	WHAT TRAINER/MENTOR DOES
II. Observing How Children Learn About The World Around Them	Read about how children use their senses and other skills to explore and develop understandings about the world. Observe each child in the program at play or during a daily routine. (This may take a week or more.) Use the observation notes to answer questions about what the children might be thinking and how thinking skills develop.	During a **phone conference** or **home visit**, discuss provider's observation notes and answers to questions. Encourage provider to conduct frequent, brief observations of children to better understand what they are thinking and how they are learning about the world. If possible, observe during home visits, watching what children are doing and saying. Share examples with provider of how children are expanding their thinking.
III. Promoting Children's Thinking Skills	Read about techniques and strategies providers can use to help children feel confident about themselves as learners. Complete chart on how children demonstrate thinking skills.	During a **home visit**, review chart of examples recorded by provider. Observe provider and give feedback about ways to further support children's cognitive development.
IV. Providing Materials That Promote Cognitive Development	Read about ways in which the environment and materials can enhance cognitive growth. Make a toy for the children. Observe a child playing with the toy and answer questions about what the child was learning.	During a **phone conference** or **home visit**, discuss provider's answers to questions. Suggest additional toys to make for the children that would help them develop cognitive skills.

Module 5: Cognitive (Continued)

LEARNING ACTIVITY	WHAT PROVIDER DOES	WHAT TRAINER/MENTOR DOES
V. Helping Children Learn to Solve Problems	Read about the importance of problem-solving skills and what providers can do to encourage problem solving. Record interactions with children outdoors and experiences using open-ended questions. After discussing responses with trainer, repeat activity.	During a **phone conference** discuss use of open-ended questions to help children develop problem-solving skills. Discuss when it is a good idea to intervene and when it is best to allow children to solve their own problems.
Summarizing Your Progress	Review responses to pre-training assessment and summarize knowledge and skills acquired in completing this module.	During a **phone conference** discuss provider's responses; then schedule a **home visit** to complete the assessment for this module.

Strategies for Extending Learning

- Put together a portable collection of scrap materials and "beautiful junk." During home visits, help providers make new toys for their FCC home. Encourage providers to start their own collections of "beautiful junk."

- Offer a workshop on Jean Piaget's stages of cognitive development. Encourage providers to offer examples they have observed of the cognitive development of children from infancy through school-age.

- Start an FCC scrapbook with examples of things children do and say that show how they are learning to think. For example, "Small people are singing inside the tape player." Encourage providers to add examples from their own experiences. During group meetings, use these examples for a discussion of how children are making sense of their world.

- During visits to FCC homes, model ways of questioning children to extend their thinking. For example, "What would happen if I mixed the red paint with the blue finger paint?" "Why doesn't the sand fall out of the vacuum?"

- Suggest that providers assess how well the materials in their homes help the children develop cognitive skills. If they find things that are either too challenging or not challenging enough, they might want to arrange a temporary exchange with another provider. For example, if the children are no longer using the sorting box, a provider might pass it on to someone who cares for younger children who would still find this toy interesting.

Completing Module 6: Communication

LEARNING ACTIVITY	WHAT PROVIDER DOES	WHAT TRAINER/MENTOR DOES

Overview and Pre-Training Assessment	Read about the development of communication skills and about provider competence.
	
	Write brief responses to situational questions about promoting children's communication skills.
	
	Use a checklist to assess communication skills.
	
	Complete pre-training assessment and list three to five skills to improve or topics to learn more about.
		Review the ongoing written observations of provider.
		
		Discuss during a **phone conference** or **home visit**, provider's:
		
		    responses to situational questions;
		
		    self-assessment of communication skills and how this relates to promoting children's communication skills; and
		
		    pre-training assessment.
		
		Validate where possible with written observations.

I. Using Your Knowledge of Child Development to Promote Communication Skills	Read about the development of communication skills from birth through the school-age years. Write examples of ways providers promote children's communication skills.	During a **phone conference** discuss examples recorded by provider. Identify other ways provider has promoted children's communication skills. Encourage provider to add to the chart while completing the remaining learning activities.
II. Understanding How Language Skills Develop	Read about the stages of language development. Observe the language development of two children over one week. Complete an observation summary form for each child.	During a **home visit**, observe the same two children that provider is observing so you will be aware of their language development. Review and discuss each item on the language observation summaries. Compare your observations with the provider.

Module 6: Communication (Continued)

LEARNING ACTIVITY	WHAT PROVIDER DOES	WHAT TRAINER/MENTOR DOES
III. Helping Children Develop Communication Skills	Read about how providers help children learn to communicate by developing a trusting, responsive relationship with each child, preparing an environment that supports communication, and serving as a language model. Use the observation summaries from the previous activity to plan strategies and activities that will promote children's language skills. After two weeks, answer questions about the effects of the strategies and activities.	During a **phone conference** or **home visit**, discuss the provider's strategies for language development. If possible, observe provider implementing the planned activities and strategies. Provide feedback to provider and assist in redesigning or expanding the strategies or activities.
IV. Selecting and Using Books With Children	Read about selecting books for children, and review ideas for reading with each age group. Select two books (or chapter of a book) that are appropriate for the children in the program. Read the book or chapter to a child. Answer questions about the reading experience. Repeat the activity with a second book and child.	During a **phone conference** or **home visit**, suggest books that would be appropriate for the children, and ways to use books effectively. Discuss provider's experiences in reading with two children and the differences in how the children responded. Suggest that provider review the content and format of the books in the home to assess how appropriate they are for the children.
V. Promoting Children's Literacy Skills	Read about development of literacy, foundations for writing and reading, and creating an environment to promote literacy. Observe the emerging reading and writing skills of a child and assess the environment for literacy promotion.	During a **phone conference** or **home visit**, discuss how children develop reading and writing skills. Review and discuss provider's observation summary. Help provider note new ways to include literacy-building materials.

Module 6: Communication (Continued)

LEARNING ACTIVITY	WHAT PROVIDER DOES	WHAT TRAINER/MENTOR DOES
Summarizing Your Progress	Review responses to pre-training assessment and summarize knowledge and skills acquired in completing this module.	During a **phone conference** discuss provider's responses; then schedule a **home visit** to complete the assessment for this module.

Strategies for Extending Learning

• Ask providers if you may tape-record them during home visits so that they can hear how they talk to children. Listen to the tape together and discuss ways to promote children's communication skills.

• Have providers identify children who may have a speech or language delay. Work with them to develop supportive activities. Help the provider identify an appropriate referral for the family if needed.

• Suggest that providers use family photos to make books for the children. Books for younger children might include pictures covered with clear Contact paper. Books for older children might include their own comments about the pictures. Given pictures and other materials, school-age children could make their own books or could help make books for the younger children.

• Suggest that providers keep track for one day of all the times they use and model literacy skills such as reading and writing, for example, beginning in the morning when they remind families to sign in. Have them review their daily logs and think of ways to include the children in literacy activities.

Completing Module 7: Creative

LEARNING ACTIVITY	WHAT PROVIDER DOES	WHAT TRAINER/MENTOR DOES

Overview and Pre-Training Assessment	Read about creativity and provider competence.
	
	Write brief responses to situational questions about promoting creativity.
	
	Complete several exercises to stimulate creative thinking.
	
	Complete pre-training assessment and list three to five skills to improve or topics to learn more about.
		Review the ongoing written observations of provider.
		
		Discuss during a **phone conference** or **home visit** provider's:
		
		    responses to situational questions;
		
		    experiences with creative thinking exercises and how they relate to encouraging children's creativity; and
		
		    pre-training assessment.
		
		Validate where possible with written observations.

I. Encouraging Children's Creativity Throughout the Day	Read about how children develop creativity. Keep a log for three days, documenting examples of how children's creativity was encouraged.	During a **home visit**, review provider's activity form on promoting creativity. Share your observations of how provider promoted creativity. Encourage provider to add to the chart.

Module 7: Creative (Continued)

LEARNING ACTIVITY	WHAT PROVIDER DOES	WHAT TRAINER/MENTOR DOES
II. Using Music and Movement Experiences to Promote Creativity	Read about how children respond to music and movement and different ways provider can incorporate music and movement into everyday activities. Plan and implement a music or movement activity. Answer questions about how the activity encouraged creativity and what changes to make before trying the activity again.	During a **phone conference** or **home visit**, encourage provider to continue planning and implementing simple music and movement experiences. Discuss the variety of ways music and movement can be incorporated throughout the day. If asked, assist the provider in planning the activity. If possible, observe provider conducting the activity and provide feedback.
III. Planning Art Experiences That Promote Creativity	Read about the different kinds of art experiences and how to plan successful art activities for children of various ages. Complete an art supplies inventory. Observe and take notes on one child participating in art activities over a three day period. Plan and implement an art activity based on the child's interests and skills. Answer questions about the planned activity, what happened when it was implemented, and what changes might be made before trying it again.	If asked, assist the provider in observing the child or planning the activity. Discuss what provider learned about this child's interests and skills. If possible, observe provider conducting the activity and provide feedback. During a **phone conference** or **home visit**, discuss the art experience planned, what happened, whether it matched the level of child(ren) observed, and how provider encouraged creativity. Encourage provider to continue planning and implementing creative art activities. If appropriate, help provider feel comfortable with planning and implementing messy activities. Help provider collect materials children can use in art activities.

Module 7: Creative (Continued)

LEARNING ACTIVITY	WHAT PROVIDER DOES	WHAT TRAINER/MENTOR DOES
IV. Using Sand and Water to Promote Creativity	Read about introducing sand and water play and providing props that will extend children's enjoyment of these materials. Plan and implement a sand or water play activity for all of the children in care. Answer questions about the planned activity, what happened when it was implemented, and what changes might be made before trying it again.	During a **phone conference** or **home visit**, help provider find ways to include sand and water play in the daily schedule as often as possible. If possible, observe provider conducting the activity and provide feedback. Help provider collect props for sand and water play. Help clean up after a messy activity; model ways to include children in cleanup.
Summarizing Your Progress	Review responses to pre-training assessment and summarize knowledge and skills acquired in completing this module.	During a **phone conference** discuss provider's responses; then schedule a **home visit** to complete the assessment for this module.

Strategies for Extending Learning

- Role-play with providers ways to explain to families that young children enjoy the *process* of creating more than their products. Help providers plan a family workshop to show why worksheets and prepared art activities are inappropriate for children. Families could color a page from a coloring book and then make anything they want using a wide variety of art and collage materials. Providers could lead a discussion about how people felt during and after each activity.

- Conduct a hands-on workshop and have providers experience different art, music and movement, sand, and water activities. It's fun, and participants realize that the mess and noise is worth the experience.

- Help providers find space in their homes to store projects that children want to work on for days or weeks at a time.

- Ask providers to keep records of each child's creative activities. Encourage providers to write examples of the child's creative thinking or problem solving. Records can be reviewed periodically to prepare for a family conference or to assess the child's development.

- Take photographs of the children when they are engaged in creative experiences. Suggest that providers create an attractive display of these pictures and, if appropriate, a variety of children's creations. Pictures can be changed monthly.

Completing Module 8: Self

LEARNING ACTIVITY	WHAT PROVIDER DOES	WHAT TRAINER/MENTOR DOES
Overview and Pre-Training Assessment	Read about sense of self and provider competence. Write brief responses to situational questions about building children's sense of self. Answer questions about a personal school experience that helped build a positive sense of self. Complete pre-training assessment and list three to five skills to improve or topics to learn more about.	Review the ongoing written observations of provider. Discuss during a **phone conference** or **home visit** provider's: responses to situational questions; experiences with a teacher who promoted the provider's sense of self and how this relates to helping children develop a sense of self; and pre-training assessment. Validate where possible with written observations.
I. Using Age-Appropriate Approaches to Build Children's Sense of Self	Read about how providers can promote children's sense of self. Provide examples of typical behavior at different ages and how providers can support each child's sense of self.	During a **phone conference**, discuss the importance of sense of self and the various stages of development. Review provider's activity on getting to know child. Encourage provider to continue to think about ways to help promote every child's sense of self

Module 8: Self (Continued)

LEARNING ACTIVITY	WHAT PROVIDER DOES	WHAT TRAINER/MENTOR DOES
II. Getting to Know Each Child	Read about understanding individual children's behavior. Select a child whose behavior the provider does not understand or finds problematic. Answer questions about the child's behavior. Plan and use three strategies for getting to know the child. Try the strategies for a week. Summarize insights gained and how this information can be used to build the child's sense of self.	During a **phone conference** or **home visit**, discuss provider's answers to questions about the child. Share your own observations if appropriate. Discuss provider's strategies and why they were or were not successful. Encourage provider to get to know all the children and recognize personal feelings about the children.
III. Helping Children Deal With Separation	Read about how children respond to separation in various stages of development and ways providers can help them handle separation. Focus on two children who are very different from each other. Answer questions related to how each child deals with separation.	During a **phone conference** or **home visit**, discuss provider's responses and what strategies help children handle separation. If possible, observe the program and note how the provider helps children deal with their feelings about separation. Discuss the notes and provide feedback. Emphasize that children's feelings about separation arise throughout the day, not just at drop-off and pick-up times. Explain that dealing with separation is a lifelong task.

Module 8: Self (Continued)

LEARNING ACTIVITY	WHAT PROVIDER DOES	WHAT TRAINER/MENTOR DOES
IV. Using Caring Language To Help Build Children's Sense of Self	Read about the importance of talking to children in caring ways that help build sense of self. Write caring language a provider might use to respond to a child in different situations.	During a **home visit**, acknowledge provider's use of caring language. Some providers may need a lot of encouragement and feedback as they begin to use caring language. Offer feedback and model use of caring language during this and future home visits. Discuss provider's written examples of caring language for different situations. Encourage provider to make and display several signs listing caring language to use as reminders.
V. Providing Appropriate Support for Children	Read about importance of getting to recognize and know when children do and do not need assistance. Keep a diary of support provided to two children during a five-day period.	During a **phone conference** or **home visit**, discuss with provider some ways to help children feel competent and successful. Review and give feedback on the provider's diary. Encourage provider to continue with observations and offer suggestions of ways to offer additional support to children.

Module 8: Self (Continued)

LEARNING ACTIVITY	WHAT PROVIDER DOES	WHAT TRAINER/MENTOR DOES
VI. Providing an Environment That Promotes Success	Read about the physical environment and its impact on building a sense of self. Complete chart on the materials that help build children's sense of self.	During a **phone conference** or **home visit**, discuss with provider ways to change the environment to help children learn and build skills. Review provider's chart and offer suggestions for adding to it.
Summarizing Your Progress	Review responses to pre-training assessment and summarize knowledge and skills acquired in completing this module.	During a **phone conference** discuss provider's responses; then schedule a **home visit** to complete the assessment for this module.

Strategies for Extending Learning

- Discuss materials that providers would like to add to the FCC home to offer greater challenges, encourage children to use skills, and provide greater variety.

- Provide materials such as markers and large index cards for providers to make signs to remind them of what they can say to children to encourage a sense of self. Signs can include phrases appropriate for different rooms in the house. For example, a sign in the bathroom might say, "You used the toilet all by yourself, and you remembered to flush." A poster next to the kitchen table might say, "You tasted everything you put on your plate."

- Find out about agencies that offer workshops for families and providers on how a positive sense of self can help children resist drug and alcohol abuse when they get older.

- Suggest having children make books depicting what they do at the FCC home. Books can be illustrated with children's drawings, photographs, or a combination of the two.

Completing Module 9: Social

LEARNING ACTIVITY	WHAT PROVIDER DOES	WHAT TRAINER/MENTOR DOES
Overview and Pre-Training Assessment	Read about social development and provider competence. Write brief responses to situational questions about social development. Give examples of how provider uses and models social skills. Complete pre-training assessment and list three to five skills to improve or topics to learn more about.	Review the ongoing written observations of provider. Discuss during a **phone conference** or **home visit** provider's: responses to situational questions; experiences using and modeling social skills and what children can learn; and pre-training assessment. Validate where possible with written observations.
I. Using Age-Appropriate Approaches to Promote Social Development	Read about how infants, toddlers, preschoolers, and school-age children learn to relate to others and what providers can do to encourage social development. Read sample situations and suggest appropriate provider responses.	During a **phone conference** or **home visit**, discuss provider's responses. Share your observations of instances when provider promoted children's social development.

Module 9: Social (Continued)

LEARNING ACTIVITY	WHAT PROVIDER DOES	WHAT TRAINER/MENTOR DOES
II. Creating an Environment That Supports Social Development	Read about setting up the environment to make group living comfortable and answer questions about providing space for children to be alone. Read about encouraging children to play with others, creating space for dramatic play, and encouraging play through the use of prop boxes. Create and use a prop box, and write about what happened when it was used by the children. Develop a plan for creating two more prop boxes.	During a **home visit**, discuss how provider has arranged the environment so children have the option of being alone or in a group. Offer to assist provider in collecting items for prop boxes; encourage provider to involve families in collecting props. Discuss completed prop box plan and report; offer suggestions on how to extend children's play. Encourage provider to create prop boxes that relate to the unique interests of children and to the community in which they live.
III. Encouraging Children's Play	Read about how children of different ages play and what providers can do to encourage children's social development through play. Observe pretend or dramatic play of several children during free play for at least half an hour. Answer questions about the observation, the social skills demonstrated, and the provider's role in extending children's play. Review observation notes and plan ways to extend children's play.	During a **phone conference** or **home visit**, discuss completed observation notes; discuss other ways to extend play, and offer suggestions on methods that were not successful. Discuss the kinds of pretend and dramatic play provider has noticed children of different ages engaged in and props that would extend children's play. Discuss ways to build on children's interests for an extended period of time.

Module 9: Social (Continued)

LEARNING ACTIVITY	WHAT PROVIDER DOES	WHAT TRAINER/MENTOR DOES
IV. Helping Children Learn Caring Behaviors	Read about how to recognize and encourage children's caring behaviors. Observe children and record examples of how they use prosocial behaviors. Note examples of how provider demonstrates and promotes caring behaviors. Make a book about some of the children's caring behaviors and read it with the children. Involve older children in making the book.	During a **phone conference** or **home visit**, discuss observation summary and discuss ways to further encourage children's prosocial behaviors. Share examples you have seen of how provider encourages children to help each other. Discuss book with provider and think of other topics for additional books that provider or older children might make.
V. Helping Children Relate Positively to Others	Read about provider's role in helping all children (especially shy, aggressive, or rejected children) make friends. Observe a child who needs help learning to make friends. Develop and implement a plan for helping the child relate to others. Describe the results after two weeks.	During a **phone conference** or **home visit**, discuss children who may be having trouble making friends. Review provider's observation notes, plan, and results; offer feedback and suggestions. Discuss with provider the importance of helping children learn how to make friends. Encourage provider to intervene with children who need assistance.
Summarizing Your Progress	Review responses to pre-training assessment and summarize knowledge and skills acquired in completing this module.	During a **phone conference** discuss provider's responses; then schedule a **home visit** to complete the assessment for this module.

Strategies for Extending Learning

- Invite providers to share with each other the props and materials they provide to encourage pretend and dramatic play.

- Offer a workshop on play, highlighting the book *Facilitating Play* by Sara Smilansky and Leah Shefatya. Explain their ideas about the importance of play and about adults' roles in supporting children's play.

- Assist providers who want to work with families to locate professional help for a child who seems to have severe problems getting along with others.

- Share journal articles and other professional resources (such as those written by Lilian Katz) and children's books on topics related to social development.

Completing Module 10: Guidance

LEARNING ACTIVITY	WHAT PROVIDER DOES	WHAT TRAINER/MENTOR DOES
Overview and Pre-Training Assessment	Read about the importance of helping children develop self-control and examples of provider competence. Write brief responses to situational questions about helping children develop self-control. Answer questions about personal self-discipline and self-control. Complete pre-training assessment and list three to five skills to improve or topics to learn more about.	Review the ongoing written observations of provider. Discuss during **phone conference** or **home visit** provider's: responses to situational questions; personal experience with losing control and how this relates to what children need to gain self-control; and pre-training assessment. Validate where possible with written observations.
I. Using Positive Approaches to Guide Children's Behavior	Read about the differences between discipline and punishment and the understandings that are the basis for positive discipline strategies. Read about characteristics of children of different ages and how providers can guide their behavior in positive ways. Write examples of typical child behaviors and positive guidance approaches that providers might use.	During **phone conference** or **home visit**, discuss the differences between discipline and punishment. Make sure provider understands why it is important to help children develop self-control. Review positive guidance examples recorded by provider. Share your observations of instances when provider used positive guidance techniques.

Module 10: Guidance (Continued)

LEARNING ACTIVITY	WHAT PROVIDER DOES	WHAT TRAINER/MENTOR DOES
II. Arranging Your Home to Promote Self-Control	Consider how the environment and the way materials are organized affect the children's and provider's behavior. Complete a chart about five common behavior problems, possible problems in the environment, and ways to make changes to help alleviate the problem behaviors. Think about the children in care and whether they exhibit any common behavior problems. Decide if there is a need to change the environment.	During **home visit**, encourage provider to consider the environment as a way to promote positive behavior. Review completed chart and analysis of the environment. Discuss how the proposed changes will improve children's behavior. Help provider make changes and assess results.
III. Using Language to Provide Positive Guidance	Read about how to use positive language to promote self-control. Review a chart of what a provider might say to children in different situations. Write examples of words to promote self-control in different situations. Write language examples on a chart and hang in the FCC home as a reminder. (optional)	During **phone conference** or **home visit**, review and give feedback on provider's examples. Encourage positive approaches and discuss those that are inappropriate. Ask: "How might a child feel if you said ...?" or "What might a child think if you said ...?" Acknowledge provider's understanding by giving specific examples from your observations. Suggest alternatives to negative statements you heard.

Module 10: Guidance (Continued)

LEARNING ACTIVITY	WHAT PROVIDER DOES	WHAT TRAINER/MENTOR DOES
IV. Setting Rules and Limits	Read about what to consider and how to involve children in setting rules and limits. Read a chart about ineffective and effective ways to remind children of rules and limits. List examples of the limits established for children. Analyze one rule: its purpose, how it is individualized, and how it is communicated.	During **phone conference** or **home visit**, review and discuss provider's examples of limits and analysis of one rule. Discuss how provider makes sure that the rules and limits are based on her knowledge of child development and are revised to meet changing needs.
V. Responding to Problem Behaviors	Read about challenging behaviors such as temper tantrums and biting that children sometimes use to express feelings. Think of a child who has a challenging behavior. Describe the child's behavior and how the provider responds. Talk with the child's family and develop a plan for responding to the behavior. Implement the plan and evaluate the results.	Discuss the meaning of "problem behavior" and why this term is used instead of "problem child." If asked, help provider prepare for discussion with the child's family. If possible, during a **home visit**, observe the child with the problem behavior and share your notes with provider. Support provider in implementing the strategy for dealing with the problem behavior. Regularly discuss whether the strategy is helping. Reinforce provider's continued use of positive guidance to respond to problem behaviors.
Summarizing Your Progress	Review responses to pre-training assessment and summarize knowledge and skills acquired in completing this module.	During a **phone conference**, discuss provider's responses; then schedule a **home visit** to complete their assessments in this module.

Module 10: Guidance (Continued)

Strategies for Extending Learning

- Arrange for providers to visit homes of others providers who are using positive guidance techniques. Ask providers to write observation notes and discuss the observations.

- Sponsor a workshop for families and providers to discuss typical behaviors of children and appropriate positive guidance techniques that can be used at home. Help providers to plan an agenda and decide the key ideas to be shared with families.

- Ask providers if you may tape-record their conversations and interactions with children. Listen to the tape together to identify language used to guide children's behavior. Providers may use the tape recorder for an additional week to monitor their interactions with children.

- Have providers role-play responses to challenging behaviors such as hitting, lying, talking back, or biting. (The role plays should address the provider's immediate response to the child, as opposed to the long term strategies they would use to find the cause of the behavior and to address it.)

- Have providers discuss and debate the pros and cons of using "time-out" as a guidance technique. Summarize why most providers use the technique inappropriately. For example, time out is meant to be used in a matter-of-fact way, without threats to children. Instead, many adults threaten children with time out and administer it as they would a punishment. "If you don't pick up those toys right now, you're going to get a time out."

Completing Module 11: Families

LEARNING ACTIVITY	WHAT PROVIDER DOES	WHAT TRAINER/MENTOR DOES

Overview and Pre-Training Assessment	Read about how providers and families work as a team and about provider competence.
	
	Write brief responses to situational questions about working with families.
	
	Answer questions about personal family experiences and compare them to today's families.
	
	Complete pre-training assessment and list three to five skills to improve or topics to learn more about.
		Review the ongoing written observations of provider.
		
		Discuss during **phone conference** or **home visit** provider's:
		
		    responses to situational questions;
		
		    experiences growing up in a family and how they affect developing a partnership with families; and
		
		    pre-training assessment.
		
		Validate where possible with written observations.

I. Developing Partnerships With Families	Read about the initial meeting with families, maintaining strong partnerships with families, and keeping them informed about the program. Tape or take notes on interactions with families for three days and note ways of supporting a partnership.	During a **phone conference** or **home visit**, discuss how provider keeps families informed about the program. Read newsletters, notices, and so forth, and discuss tone, language level, and cultural sensitivity. Observe provider interacting with families; give an objective account of what was said and the nonverbal communication that took place. Listen to tape, if applicable, and review provider's notes on maintaining strong partnership. Give feedback and make suggestions for improving relationships, if necessary.

Module 11: Families (Continued)

LEARNING ACTIVITY	WHAT PROVIDER DOES	WHAT TRAINER/MENTOR DOES
II. Working Together to Support Children	Read about the different kinds of information families and providers can share about a child. Select a child and family to learn more about. Let the family know they have been selected. For two weeks, record daily communications with the family, including information shared. At the end of each week, summarize what information was shared and how it helped meet the child's needs. Discuss the activity with the parents.	During a **phone conference** or **home visit**, help provider learn ways to help families be "experts" rather than seeing the provider as the "expert." Discuss how this activity helped provider meet the child's needs. If possible, observe provider interacting with selected family; give an objective account of what was said and the nonverbal communication that took place. Suggest that provider complete an abbreviated version of the activity with the families of other children in the group in order to get to know them better.
III. Offering Ways for Families to Be Involved	Read suggestions for helping families become more involved with the FCC program. Plan and implement a family-involvement strategy. Review the results of the strategy and develop plans to follow up.	During a **phone conference**, encourage provider to ask families for ideas. Review provider's written strategy; provide feedback. Offer to help get supplies if needed. Discuss different types of family involvement and help set realistic expectations.

Module 11: Families (Continued)

LEARNING ACTIVITY	WHAT PROVIDER DOES	WHAT TRAINER/MENTOR DOES
IV. Planning and Participating in Conferences With Families	Read about the goals of conferences and how to plan and participate in them. Complete a conference planning form and conduct the conference. Complete a conference evaluation form, summarizing what happened, information shared, and what might be done differently next time.	During a **phone conference** or **home visit**, discuss the importance of holding regular conferences to discuss a child in depth. Help provider prepare for the conference by role-playing what will take place. If possible, attend the conference and give feedback on the information presented, tone, body language, and overall success of the interaction. Discuss provider's ideas and feelings about what took place. Help provider practice several communication techniques.
V. Resolving Differences	Read about how to resolve differences in ways that strengthen partnerships with families. Read three case studies of how differences between families and providers were handled. Describe different responses to situations when providers and families have differences or misunderstandings.	During a **phone conference** or **home visit**, help provider understand that it is normal for providers and families occasionally to disagree about caregiving practices. Discuss case studies with provider. Ask, "How would you have responded in this situation?" Discuss situations when provider disagreed with a family and how it was handled.

Module 11: Families (Continued)

LEARNING ACTIVITY	WHAT PROVIDER DOES	WHAT TRAINER/MENTOR DOES
VI. Providing Support to Families	Read about recognizing and responding to families who are under stress.

Note examples of times when provider reached out to families in response to requests or because they appeared to need support.

Describe the problem, the family's request or need, the response, and the outcome. | During a **phone conference** or **home visit**, review examples, offer feedback, and answer provider's questions about supporting families under stress. Emphasize policies on referrals and confidentiality.

Discuss how to look for signs of children's stress.

Discuss limits of provider's role and when to refer a family for professional assistance. |
| Summarizing Your Progress | Review responses to pre-training assessment and summarize knowledge and skills acquired in completing this module. | During a **phone conference** discuss provider's responses; then schedule a **home visit** to complete the assessment for this module. |

Strategies for Extending Learning

- Lead a discussion on similarities and differences between providers' childhood families and today's families (from the module overview). Provide statistics that describe today's families—for example, how many parents are single parents, how many families include two working spouses, how many families include children from previous marriages, and how many families live far away from their own parents and siblings.

- Have providers role-play a conference with a family, handling an angry parent, or resolving differences. Have the group provide feedback and additional ideas.

- Develop a list of community organizations for family referrals (e.g., hotlines and support groups).

- Provide information on signs and symptoms of various problems (drug use, spousal abuse, depression) so providers are aware of them. Ask representatives from appropriate agencies to make a presentation on how to respond when they suspect that a family has a problem that needs to be addressed.

Module 11: Families (Continued)

- Conduct a survey of all FCC families to find out what kinds of information they would like to receive from the program and in what form (e.g., newsletters, informal chats, bulletin board). The survey can also ask families what information about their children they would like to share with providers.

- Work with providers to develop a handout for families that outlines the foundations of literacy and explains how families can help children develop reading and writing skills during their daily routines and activities at home.

Completing Module 12: Program Management

LEARNING ACTIVITY	WHAT PROVIDER DOES	WHAT TRAINER/MENTOR DOES
Overview and Pre-Training Assessment	Read about provider competence in program management and the various roles providers must assume. Complete a chart listing common frustrating situations and plans to improve them. Complete pre-training assessment and list three to five skills to improve or topics to learn more about.	Review the written observations of provider. Discuss during **phone conference** or **home visit** provider's: responses to situational questions; completed chart about frustrating situations; and pre-training assessment. Validate where possible from your own knowledge of the FCC home's operations.
I. Using a Systematic Approach to Observing and Taking Notes	Read why providers conduct observations. Review guidelines for observing children systematically and examples of good and bad observation notes. Select a child to observe daily for a two-week period. Arrange for trainer to observe the child at the same time at least once. Compare records after the co-observation and after two weeks.	During a **home visit**, conduct (and then discuss) at least one observation of the child at the same time that the provider is observing. Discuss examples of provider's accurate and objective notes. Help provider rewrite inappropriate notes so they are accurate and objective.

Module 12: Program Management (Continued)

LEARNING ACTIVITY	WHAT PROVIDER DOES	WHAT TRAINER/MENTOR DOES
II. Offering a Program That Meets Each Child's Needs	Read about the importance of providing a program that responds to each child as an individual. Observe two children (preferably of different age groups) at least once a day over a two-week period. Review observation notes and use them to complete an Individualization Summary Form for each child. Use the forms for all the children in the program.	During a **home visit**, offer to care for children while provider practices observing and taking notes. Help provider draw conclusions about children's strengths, interests, and needs. Discuss the completed forms and plans for meeting the child's individual needs. Encourage provider to establish a system for regularly observing all the children.
III. Planning the Program	Read about the importance of long-range and weekly planning, what guides the planning process, how planning is done, and evaluating the program. Review a sample planning form; then develop a weekly plan. Use the plan for one week; then answer questions to evaluate how it worked.	During a **phone conference** or **home visit**, review and provide feedback on the provider's weekly plan. Read and discuss responses to the evaluation questions. Ask how the plan provided enough flexibility to meet children's individual needs.

Module 12: Program Management (Continued)

LEARNING ACTIVITY	WHAT PROVIDER DOES	WHAT TRAINER/MENTOR DOES
IV. Running a Family Child Care Business	Read about establishing sound business practices, including complying with laws and regulations, developing policies and procedures, and maintaining accurate records. Evaluate effectiveness of existing policies and procedures. Identify need for improvement in maintaining records. Review sample interview, enrollment and permission forms that can be modified or used in the FCC home.	During a **phone conference** discuss the policies and procedures a provider has in place and any others that may be useful. Discuss laws and regulations that are specific to the provider's community. Share samples of contracts used by providers in the area. Discuss provider's responses to policies and procedures activity. Help provider plan and implement any needed changes.
Summarizing Your Progress	Review responses to pre-training assessment and summarize knowledge and skills acquired in completing this module.	During a **phone conference**, discuss provider's responses; then schedule a **home visit** to complete the module assessment.

Strategies for Extending Learning

- Ask providers to help plan and conduct a workshop on time-management skills and record keeping techniques.

- Introduce providers to a variety of observation and documenting formats, such as time sampling, event sampling, rating scales, and skills checklists. Encourage them to pick an instrument or format that serves a particular need—observing to see if the environment is working, noting children's developmental progress, keeping records to discuss with parents, and so on.

- Provide a video camera for providers to set up in their homes. Encourage providers to let the camera run, cinema-verité style. Then meet with the provider to view what the camera has recorded. Discuss what the children did, materials and skills they used, how they interacted with each other and with the provider, and how the provider responded.

Module 12: Program Management (Continued)

- Help providers establish practical systems for storing information about individual children, professional resources, business records, and FCC home policies. Encourage providers to maintain calendars for regularly observing children, the environment, and how children play together.

- Have providers discuss how they can individualize activities while still including all of the children in that activity, for example, preparing lunch, taking a walk in the neighborhood, or blowing bubbles outdoors.

Completing Module 13: Professionalism

LEARNING ACTIVITY	WHAT PROVIDER DOES	WHAT TRAINER/MENTOR DOES

Overview and Pre-Training Assessment	Read about what it means to be a professional and the stages providers pass through as they become committed professionals.
	
	Write brief responses to situational questions about a provider's demonstrated professionalism.
	
	Respond to questions about being a provider and aspirations for the future.
	
	Complete pre-training assessment and list three to five skills to improve or topics to learn more about.
		Review the written observations of providers.
		
		During a **phone conference** or **home visit**, discuss provider's:
		
		    responses to situational questions;
		
		    feelings about being a provider and aspirations; and
		
		    pre-training assessment.
		
		Validate where possible from meetings and your knowledge of provider.

I. Examining Your Practices	Complete two readings about being an early childhood professional. Think about and respond to questions about individual interests and abilities. Discuss responses to the questions with two colleagues. Write down what was learned from the exercise. Read about standards of the child care profession and write a response to one area of interest discussed in NAEYC's *Developmentally Appropriate Practice*.	Supply copy of NAEYC's *Developmentally Appropriate Practice*. During a **phone conference**, discuss past observations when you saw provider share personal interests with the children, and discuss their reactions. Identify provider's other interests and strengths and discuss how they can be applied to work. Discuss provider's reactions to the NAEYC statement.

Module 13: Professionalism (Continued)

LEARNING ACTIVITY	WHAT PROVIDER DOES	WHAT TRAINER/MENTOR DOES
II. Continuing to Learn About Caring for Children	Read about joining professional organizations and other ways to continue professional growth. Review answers to the section in a previous learning activity. Select one item from responses to "I would like to be better at" or "I would like to know more about." Develop a plan to learn more about this item, including sources and contact persons. Read about making plans for continued learning. Develop short- and long-range plans for professional development.	During a **phone conference**, discuss provider's plans for professional development. Provide information about professional organizations. Help provider identify ways to undertake training and skill development. Inform provider of upcoming classes, lectures, and conferences. Periodically review progress on reaching goals, and provide reinforcement and assistance.
III. Behaving Ethically in Your Work	Review examples of family child care ethics and of professional and unprofessional behaviors related to these ethics. Write examples of professional behavior related to the ethics of family child care. Write brief responses to three ethical case studies.	During a **home visit**, discuss the ethical case studies. Stress that there are difficult situations without easy answers. Point out examples of provider's ethical behavior. Continue discussions of issues as they arise. Acknowledge provider's conscientious work habits and ethical behavior.

Module 13: Professionalism (Continued)

LEARNING ACTIVITY	WHAT PROVIDER DOES	WHAT TRAINER/MENTOR DOES
IV. Becoming an Advocate for Children and Families	Read about how providers can be advocates for children. Develop a plan for becoming an advocate for children and families.	During a **phone conference** or **home visit**, discuss current issues with provider. Collect articles and bulletins to share with provider. Discuss plans and offer to assist provider in advocacy efforts. Follow up with information on major issues.
V. Taking Care of Yourself	Read about the importance of taking care of oneself. For two days, complete self-assessment on physical, emotional, and social well-being. Write a brief plan for taking care of herself.	During a **phone conference** or **home visit**, reinforce the importance of taking care of oneself. Review provider's plans and offer assistance in implementing them. Be a good model by taking care of yourself.
Summarizing Your Progress	Review responses to pre-training assessment and summarize knowledge and skills acquired in completing this module.	During a **phone conference**, discuss provider's responses; then schedule a **home visit** to complete the assessment for this module.

Strategies for Extending Learning

- Conduct workshops on issues such as appropriate guidance methods, how to work with families who disagree with the FCC home's practices, or other topics that providers identify as problem areas.

- Hold a discussion about current issues affecting children in the community or state, and discuss ways in which FCC providers can become more involved in advocacy efforts.

- Provide information on professional organizations and encourage providers to join at least one.

- Build a lending library of professional books, journals, and audiovisual materials.

Module 13: Professionalism (Continued)

- Find out about classes on stress management, nutrition, assertiveness, or other topics relevant to a provider's well-being, and share these materials.

- Plan and implement a training program for providers who would like to serve as mentors for other providers.

- Encourage providers to become partners to support each other's professional development. Providers can share rides, care for each other's children at night or on the weekends, plan and lead workshops together, share resources, and otherwise help each other reach professional goals.

- Discuss with providers the next steps in their professional development: college courses, seeking accreditation from the National Association for Family Child Care, becoming a CDA candidate in training, or continued self-study. Help providers see how the modules fit their professional growth.

IV. Assessing Each Provider's Progress

IV. Assessing Each Provider's Progress

This chapter includes the knowledge and competency assessments for the 13 modules in *Caring for Children in Family Child Care*. Trainers administer these assessments after providers have successfully completed all parts of a module—the overview, the learning activities, and summarizing progress. The *knowledge assessment* validates the provider's understanding of the information presented in the module; the *competency assessment* allows the provider to demonstrate competence by using relevant strategies to care for children.

Having provided feedback on all the learning activities, you will have a good idea if a provider is ready for assessment. (If a provider is not ready for assessment, you might suggest repeating one or more of the learning activities or reviewing additional training resources.) During the final home visit for the module, give the provider a copy of the competency assessment criteria (included in this chapter after each knowledge assessment). Then, during your phone conference for "Summarizing Your Progress," discuss these criteria and whether the provider is ready for assessment. If the decision is to go ahead with the assessments, schedule a convenient time for an **assessment home visit**, during which you will administer the knowledge and competency assessments.

It is best to schedule the assessment home visit to coincide with rest time. The provider can take the knowledge assessment while the children are sleeping or resting. You can conduct the competency assessment observation in the morning or afternoon, depending on the day's activities and the skills being observed, and provide feedback on both assessments immediately or the next day. Depending on your schedule, you may want to complete the competency assessment for several modules at one time. For example, you could complete the competency assessment observation for Safe and Healthy during one extended home visit (about 2 hours), rather than making two shorter visits.

The assessment process is designed to be one more step in the learning process. If necessary, try to alleviate the provider's "test anxiety." Explain that if either assessment is not completed successfully, you will continue to assist in developing the necessary competencies.

You will need to maintain a supply of the assessments, so it might be helpful to set up a filing system for storing copies of the assessments and answer sheets.

Knowledge Assessments

The knowledge assessments are paper-and-pencil exercises that test the provider's knowledge of the information and concepts presented in the module. The questions are in true/false, multiple-choice, matching, and short-answer formats and are based on the text of the overview and learning activities.

Providers will need approximately 20 to 30 minutes of uninterrupted time (for example, during rest time, as suggested above) to complete the knowledge assessment. If you know a provider may have trouble reading the test and writing answers, you can offer assistance by reading the questions and writing down the responses.

Depending on the timing of the assessment home visit, the knowledge assessment can be administered before or after the competency assessment.

Competency Assessments

Modules 1 through 11 include a competency assessment as part of the assessment process. Modules 12 and 13 have knowledge assessments only, because mastery of the content of these modules cannot be readily observed during a single observation period. Competency assessments are scheduled times when you complete written observations of the provider working with children. You then use your observation notes to determine whether the provider has demonstrated competence.

The competency assessment criteria given to providers includes the indicators trainers will use to determine successful completion of the module. These indicators, which are drawn primarily from the pre-training assessment, address the skills covered in the module. They consist of behaviors that are observable and measurable.

Appendix C contains trainer observation forms for the competency assessments. These forms may be used when observing providers during the competency assessment process. The forms for each module include two pages for notes, followed by a list of assessment criteria. There are spaces to indicate whether each criteria has been met, partially met, or not met.

The competency assessments for Modules 1, 2, 3, and 10 include several items related to the environment and procedures that are assessed by reviewing documentation, looking at the parts of the home used by children, and questioning the provider. These should be assessed immediately before the observation period.

The recommended observation period is one hour, but it may vary according to the time of the day, what the children are doing, the scheduled and unscheduled activities that take place, and the number of modules being assessed. You may want to observe at a particular time of day so you can witness a specific routine or activity (for example, you might want to observe lunch time or outdoor play). The competency assessment for Module 11: Families should be conducted during either drop-off or pick-up times.

Observing the Provider With Children

Your documentation of the observation is an important aspect of the competency assessment. It should provide a picture of how the provider interacts with and responds to children. You will not be able to capture everything that takes place, but the more complete your observation notes, the more data you will have to determine competence. Your observation notes should provide an objective description of what happened that you can share with the provider. To be useful, observation notes should have the following characteristics:

- **Objectivity:** Include only the facts about what happens, not labels, judgments, or inferences. Record only what the provider does and says and what the children do and say.

- **Specificity:** Record as much information as possible to present a picture of the provider's practices. Include details such as the number of children involved, where in the home or outdoors the action is taking place, words and tone of voice used.

- **Accuracy:** Record the provider's and children's actions, vocalizations, and language directly and in the order in which they happen. Try to include direct quotations whenever possible.

- **Completeness:** Include descriptions of activities from beginning to end. Record information about the setting (the number and ages of children, where in the home or outdoors the action is taking place), what the provider does, what is said (if anything), and the children's verbal and nonverbal language.

Discussing the Assessment Results

Most adults are eager to know the results of their work, so it is important to score the assessments and share the results with the provider as soon as possible. Ideally, this meeting will take place during the assessment home visit. If it is not possible to hold the meeting during the same home visit, try to return the next day to discuss your assessment. In this meeting you will discuss the answers to the knowledge assessment and what you saw and heard during the observation period.

The answer sheets for the knowledge assessments are found in Appendix B. Scoring for each question is indicated on the answer sheets. Some questions have more than one answer, also indicated on the answer sheets. A perfect score is 100 percent. To complete the knowledge assessment successfully, a provider must obtain a score of at least 80 percent.

When a provider does not achieve a passing score on the knowledge assessment, review the answers together. You will need to judge how much support the provider needs to understand fully the material presented in the module.

As stated earlier, the goal is to ensure competence and understanding, not simply to have the provider pass the test. You might suggest that specific learning activities in the module be reviewed, or you might provide additional resources. Ask the provider to let you know when it is convenient to schedule the assessment again.

To score the competency assessment, use your notes to determine whether each criterion of competence that you can substantiate from your observation has been met, partially met, or not met. If a criterion was not observed, it should be left blank. You will then decide whether the provider has successfully demonstrated competence. When a provider has clearly demonstrated the skills identified as the criteria for assessment, offer your congratulations and some examples of competence drawn from your notes. If you think that a provider has demonstrated some of the skills but has not thoroughly understood the information in the module, you will need to handle the meeting accordingly.

The goal of the assessment is to validate competency. Adult learners generally know when they have not demonstrated the necessary skills to complete an assessment successfully. It is not helpful to rate a provider as competent when more support and training are needed. If a skill has not been mastered, the meeting is simply an opportunity to reassess training needs and to provide additional support.

Here are some suggestions for discussing the competency assessment.

- **Begin the conference by asking for the provider's comments.** "What do you think about what took place?" "Did everything go as you had planned?" "Were there any surprises?"

- **Sort out what went well and what problems existed, if any.** "What do you think went well?" "Is there anything you will do differently?"

- **Share your observation notes with the provider.** "Let's look at my notes about what happened and see what we can learn from them."

- **Review the criteria together.** Ask the provider to assess which strategies were clearly used and which were not.

- **Rate the use of some strategies on the basis of the provider's work on the learning activities for the module.** In one observation period it will not be possible to observe all the criteria on the list. However, you will have a good idea of whether the provider has understood the information and can demonstrate knowledge and skills in working with children.

- **Give your decision and explain your reasoning.** If the provider has clearly demonstrated competence in the functional area and you are confident that the information was understood and that the provider can apply it consistently in working with children, offer your congratulations. If possible, take a few minutes to share your observations of the progress you have seen.

If you think the provider needs more support, discuss the weaknesses you identified, giving examples from your observation notes. Then decide what form of support would be most helpful and develop a plan to work together. Assure the provider that, after developing further skills, the competency assessment may be retaken.

As providers successfully complete both the knowledge and competency assessments for a module, you should update their tracking and training documentation forms. You may want to review providers' competence in using the skills developed in previous modules while working on the current module.

There may be times when your observations indicate that a provider needs to repeat a module or at least some of the learning activities in order to strengthen her practices.

The following pages contain copies of the knowledge assessments for all 13 modules and competency assessments for Modules 1 through 11. Appendix B contains answer sheets for the knowledge assessments, and Appendix C includes trainer observation forms for the competency assessments.

Knowledge Assessment
Module 1: Safe

Multiple choice exercises. Select the best answer from those given.

1. You feel safe when you know:

    a. _____ no harm will come to you.

    b. _____ you can do something to prevent dangerous situations.

    c. _____ those around you are also concerned about safety.

    d. _____ all of the above.

2. Children begin to feel safe when they:

    a. _____ can stand and walk on their own.

    b. _____ trust their parents and other adults who care for them.

    c. _____ are around strangers a lot.

    d. _____ are punished if they do dangerous things.

3. Children are not always able to prevent possible dangers, so providers should:

    a. _____ make lots of rules for children to follow.

    b. _____ keep children in infant seats, high chairs, and playpens most of the day.

    c. _____ lead the children in organized activities all day.

    d. _____ set up an environment that is safe for children to play in and explore.

4. Providers care for children of many ages. To keep all children safe, they should:

    a. _____ know the developmental stages and safety needs of children at various ages.

    b. _____ remind preschoolers and school-age children about the safety rules.

    c. _____ identify the potential safety hazards in the home for the children in their care.

    d. _____ all of the above.

5. When selecting safe toys for children, providers should ask:

   a. _____ Is it unbreakable?

   b. _____ Is it colorful and attractive to the child?

   c. _____ Does it have sharp edges, exposed nails, sharp wires, or pins?

   d. _____ Can it be swallowed by a child?

   e. _____ all of the above.

6. When walking with children in traffic, a provider should:

   a. _____ remind children of traffic safety rules.

   b. _____ allow all the children who can walk to do so.

   c. _____ let the children run ahead and wait at the corner.

   d. _____ be sure each child rides in a stroller or holds an adult's hand.

   e. _____ a and d.

   f. _____ all of the above.

On the basis of knowledge gained through this module, complete the following exercises. Some require more than one answer. Partial credit will be given. Answer each exercise as thoroughly as you can.

7. For each of the safety measures below, explain why it helps to keep children safe.

   a. Modeling ways to take safety precautions: _____

   _____

   _____

   b. Conducting monthly emergency drills: _____

   _____

   _____

   c. Reassessing the environment when a new child enrolls: _____

   _____

   _____

8. List **two** examples of items a provider should check daily to maintain safety indoors:

   1. _____

   2. _____

9. List **two** examples of items a provider should check daily to maintain safety outdoors:

    1. _____

    2. _____

10. Think of an emergency situation that might arise while caring for children, and then list **two** things you would do to keep children safe in that situation:

    Emergency situation: _____

    1. _____

    2. _____

11. For each age group listed below, give **one** example of what children are like and what providers can do to keep them safe:

    a. Infants: _____

    _____

    _____

    b. Toddlers: _____

    _____

    _____

    c. Preschoolers: _____

    _____

    _____

    d. School-age children: _____

    _____

    _____

12. When giving first aid a provider must follow these **two** rules:

    1. _____

    _____

    2. _____

    _____

13. Describe an actual emergency or stressful event that has occurred in your life. What safety precautions did you use? How did they help you or someone else get through the experience safely?

_____

_____

_____

_____

_____

_____

Competency Assessment
Module 1: Safe

Before the observation period your trainer/mentor will assess whether you use skills such as the following:

- Conducting daily and monthly safety checks indoors and outdoors, and removing or repairing unsafe items.

- Arranging the FCC home so there are clear exits.

- Organizing indoor and outdoor areas so children can move freely without bumping into things.

- Providing safe, age-appropriate toys, materials, equipment, and activities.

- Arranging toys on low, open shelves with the heaviest items on the bottom shelves.

- Maintaining a fully stocked first-aid kit.

- Stating the correct procedures to follow when there is an injury or emergency.

- Maintaining up-to-date emergency telephone numbers for all families.

- Posting emergency phone numbers for children's families, police, fire, ambulance, and poison control next to the telephone.

- Keeping electrical wires in good condition and out of children's reach.

- Storing breakable items out of children's reach.

During the observation period your trainer will assess whether you use skills such as the following:

- Conducting and documenting monthly emergency drills. (You will conduct an emergency drill as part of the competency assessment.)

- Showing children the FCC home is a safe place and that keeping them safe is important.

- Responding quickly to children in distress.

- Following a daily schedule that provides time for active and quiet play so that children do not get overtired and have injuries.

- Taking precautions in a reassuring way without overprotecting or scaring children.

- Using diagrams, pictures, and words to remind children of safety rules.

- Modeling ways to live safely and be careful throughout the day.

- Using positive guidance to redirect children from unsafe to safe activities.

- Keeping small, easily swallowed objects out of the reach of young children.

Knowledge Assessment
Module 2: Healthy

Multiple choice exercises. Select the best answer from those given.

1. Positive health habits include:

   a. _____   eating foods that are low in fat and sugar.

   b. _____   spending time with friends and family.

   c. _____   following the latest health and nutrition fads.

   d. _____   a and b.

   e. _____   all of the above.

2. Providers teach children about good health and nutrition:

   a. _____   only during planned health and nutrition education activities.

   b. _____   in the course of daily life at the FCC home.

   c. _____   by caring for children who are sick in the FCC home.

   d. _____   none of the above.

3. Because children depend on adults to keep them healthy, providers should:

   a. _____   prevent children from putting anything in their mouths.

   b. _____   never let children feed themselves.

   c. _____   plan routines and activities to meet children's health and nutrition needs.

   d. _____   prevent children from touching each other.

4. Family-style mealtimes encourage children to:

   a. _____   serve themselves and choose their own food quantities.

   b. _____   engage in conversation with everyone else.

   c. _____   participate in setting up the table and clearing the table.

   d. _____   all of the above.

On the basis of knowledge gained through this module, complete the following exercises Some require more than one answer. Partial credit will be given. Complete each exercise as thoroughly as you can.

5. Why should providers place tissues and paper towels where children can reach them?

    _____

    _____

6. Name **two** requirements providers must follow when administering medication.

    1. _____

    2. _____

7. How can a provider make a safe solution for disinfecting toys and objects (other than dishes and utensils) mouthed by children?

    _____

    _____

    _____

8. Name **one** sign that might indicate that a child is being physically abused:

    _____

9. What happens to children if nobody reports child maltreatment?

    _____

    _____

10. List **three** things a provider should do to make diapering a sanitary procedure:

    1. _____

    2. _____

    3. _____

11. List **two** ways a provider can encourage children to try new foods.

    1. _____

    2. _____

12. List **two** things you can do to improve your own health and nutrition.

    1. _____

    _____

    2. _____

    _____

13. Name **two** strategies that help maintain a healthy environment.

    1. _____

    2. _____

14. Describe **two** things a provider could do to make the kitchen more functional and safe for children.

    1. _____

    _____

    2. _____

    _____

Competency Assessment
Module 2: Healthy

Before the observation period your trainer/mentor will assess whether you use skills such as the following:

- Checking the home daily for adequate ventilation and lighting, comfortable room temperature, and good sanitation.

- Placing tissues, paper towels, and soap within children's reach.

- Arranging the diapering area and the bathroom so it is easy to keep sanitary.

- Providing a place to isolate an ill child until the parent arrives.

- Knowing the applicable laws and regulations related to reporting child abuse and neglect, and describing the signs of possible child maltreatment.

During the observation period your trainer will assess whether you use skills such as the following:

- Opening windows daily to let in fresh air (if needed during observation period).

- Cleaning and disinfecting food preparation surfaces before and after use.

- Washing hands with soap and water before children arrive, before and after eating, before and after food preparation, before and after diapering or toileting a child, after wiping a child's nose, and as necessary.

- Washing children's hands (or helping them do it themselves) with soap and water upon arrival, before and after eating, before participating in a food preparation activity, after toileting or diapering, after wiping noses, and as necessary.

- Washing and disinfecting with bleach solution toys that are mouthed or fall on the floor (at least daily).

- Serving age-appropriate, healthy foods that are low in fats, salt, and sugar and meet Child Care Food Program requirements.

- Serving relaxed, family-style meals and encouraging children to try a variety of foods.

- Holding and talking to infants while feeding them.

- Helping children learn self-help skills (toileting, feeding, and toothbrushing).

- Talking with children about ways to stay healthy.

- Providing a balanced schedule so children get enough exercise and rest.

- Taking children outdoors every day.

- Refrigerating infant bottles and foods in individual, labeled containers and discarding unused portions.

- Storing food properly, in dated containers.

- Maintaining a positive, relaxed atmosphere to reduce tension and stress.

Knowledge Assessment
Module 3: Learning Environment

Multiple choice exercises. Select the best answer from those given.

1. The learning environment includes:

   a. _____ the indoor and outdoor space in which you care for children.

   b. _____ the furniture and materials in the space.

   c. _____ the children and adults who work and play in the space.

   d. _____ the schedule and routines you follow.

   e. _____ all of the above.

2. Factors that affect the quality of the indoor environment include:

   a. _____ room size, colors, furnishings, and equipment.

   b. _____ how expensive the toys and equipment are.

   c. _____ the people in the environment.

   d. _____ a and c.

   e. _____ all of the above.

3. Equipment and materials that encourage play and exploration include:

   a. _____ toys that very young children can safely put in their mouths.

   b. _____ manipulatives, games, and puzzles that challenge but do not frustrate children.

   c. _____ materials displayed on low, open shelves so children can find them.

   d. _____ all of the above (a, b, and c).

   e. _____ whatever toys and materials children want to play with.

4. Activity areas in the FCC home should:

   a. _____ allow for traffic flow so children won't interrupt each other.

   b. _____ help children see what choices are available and how materials are to be used.

   c. _____ separate children of different ages.

   d. _____ a and b.

   e. _____ all of the above.

On the basis of knowledge gained through this module, complete the following exercises. Some require more than one answer. Partial credit will be given. Complete each exercise as thoroughly as you can.

5. List **two** examples of ways the indoor environment and **two** examples of ways the outdoor environment can be tailored to foster learning.

   a. Indoor: _____

   _____

   b. Outdoor: _____

   _____

6. List **three** examples of the kinds of toys and materials that are appropriate for each age group (infants, toddlers, preschoolers, and school-age children):

   a. Infants: _____

   _____

   b. Toddlers: _____

   _____

   c. Preschoolers: _____

   _____

   d. School-age: _____

   _____

7. What are **three** guidelines providers should consider in developing a daily plan:

   1. _____

   2. _____

   3. _____

8. List **two** routines that occur as part of an FCC program and how a provider can make these times enjoyable for both herself and the children.

   1. _____

   _____

   2. _____

   _____

9. List **three** ways a provider can plan the outdoor environment and activities to make outdoor time a safe and enjoyable part of the program.

   1. _____

   _____

   2. _____

   _____

   3. _____

   _____

10. Describe **your idea** of a pleasant environment. What makes it pleasant and why?

   _____

   _____

Matching exercises.

11. Match the following messages in the environment in the left column with the appropriate description in the right column.

   a. ____ "You belong here. You are a valued member of this community.

   (1) Pictures on walls, books, and other materials show people of different ethnic backgrounds and different kinds of families.

   b. ____ "This is a place you can trust."

   (2) Decorative items—plants, pictures, pillows are part of environment.

   c. ____ "You can do many things on your own."

   (3) Daily routines are set on an individual basis to meet each child's special needs.

   d. ____ "This is a safe place to explore and try your ideas."

   (4) There are indoor and outdoor spaces for tumbling, climbing, rolling, and other large muscle activities.

   e. ____ "This is a good place to be."

   (5) Materials are stored on low shelves so children can choose and take the things they want to use.

12. Match the following materials in the right column with the age at which they would be introduced in the left column.

   a. ____ Young infants

   (1) simple board games such as Lotto

   b. ____ School-age children

   (2) "fill and dump" toys

   c. ____ Toddlers

   (3) large crayons

   d. ____ Preschoolers

   (4) craft supplies

   e. ____ Mobile infants

   (5) wooden or plastic rattles

Competency Assessment
Module 3: Learning Environment

Before the observation period your trainer/mentor will assess whether you use skills such as the following:

- Setting up a welcoming environment with spaces for a variety of activities.

- Providing soft, cozy spaces (indoors and outdoors) where children can be alone.

- Providing open areas with a variety of surfaces for children to explore.

- Arranging indoor and outdoor areas where children can use their large muscles.

- Having child-size furniture and equipment.

- Adapting the environment, if necessary, for children with special needs.

- Planning a consistent but flexible schedule, with daily opportunities for indoor and outdoor experiences.

During the observation period your trainer will assess whether you use skills such as the following:

- Including toys and activities that include a variety of ethnicities and cultures, including those of the children in your care.

- Conveying positive messages through the arrangement of the environment (e.g., "This is a safe place"; "You belong here").

- Arranging materials so children have clear choices and are encouraged to be independent.

- Providing materials and equipment that provide challenges but allow children to be successful.

- Providing materials that are appropriate for the interests and abilities of the children in your care.

- Providing a variety of materials to encourage pretend and dramatic play, construction, small muscle development, and thinking skills.

- Adapting the schedule to meet children's individual needs.

- Adapting the schedule to take advantage of unplanned learning opportunities.

- Allowing ample time for daily routines and using them as opportunities for learning.

- Making sure all the children can be seen at all times.

Knowledge Assessment
Module 4: Physical

Multiple choice exercises. Select the best answer from those given.

1. Physical development involves:

    a. _____   the increasing ability to control large and small muscles.

    b. _____   gross motor skills such as crawling and walking.

    c. _____   fine motor skills such as holding and pinching.

    d. _____   coordinating movement.

    e. _____   all of the above.

2. The most important way a provider can encourage physical development is to:

    a. _____   provide a wide variety of toys and materials.

    b. _____   show interest and encouragement in what a child is doing.

    c. _____   have children practice physical skills until they master them.

    d. _____   take children outdoors every day.

    e. _____   a, b, and d.

    f. _____   all of the above.

On the basis of knowledge gained through this module, complete the following exercises. Some require more than one answer. Partial credit will be given. Complete each exercise as thoroughly as you can.

3. List **two** examples of how a provider can encourage a positive sense of self as children use their physical skills:

    1. _____

    2. _____

4. Why would a provider place a toy a little out of reach of a seven-month old?

    _____

    _____

    _____

5. Define fine and gross motor skills. Give an example of each.

   a. Fine motor skill: _____

   _____

   b. Gross motor skill: _____

   _____

6. Give **two** examples of ways children develop and use their fine motor skills during routines:

   1. _____

   _____

   2. _____

   _____

7. For each of the following activities, give **two** examples of gross motor play:

   a. Outdoor Play:

   1. _____

   2. _____

   b. Blocks:

   1. _____

   2. _____

   c. Music and Movement:

   1. _____

   2. _____

   d. Woodworking:

   1. _____

   2. _____

8. Give **one** reason why a provider might use outdoor play time as an opportunity to take a short run around the play yard:

   _____

   _____

9. Give **two** examples of toys and equipment that help children develop and use their gross motor skills:

    1. _____

    2. _____

10. Give **two** examples of toys or activities that help children develop eye-hand coordination:

    1. _____

    2. _____

11. List **two** things providers can do to avoid sore backs and limbs:

    1. _____

    _____

    2. _____

    _____

12. List **one** way providers can interact with children to promote physical development:

_____

_____

_____

Competency Assessment
Module 4: Physical

During the observation period your trainer/mentor will assess whether you use skills such as the following:

- Scheduling time for the children to engage in active play every day.

- Helping and encouraging children when they are learning new skills.

- Providing safe and interesting objects for children to listen to, taste, smell, look at, pick up, and put down.

- Observing and recording information about each child's physical strengths, interests, and needs.

- Helping children develop an awareness of rhythm through music and movement.

- Arranging the indoor and outdoor environment so children can move freely and safely.

- Offering a variety of materials and equipment to promote gross motor development.

- Playing indoor and outdoor noncompetitive games with children.

- Encouraging the development of self-help skills that use large muscles.

- Planning and implementing increasingly difficult activities in which large muscles are used.

- Deciding when to intervene directly and when to let a child work out a problem.

- Offering a variety of materials that require children to use their small muscles.

- Providing opportunities for children to develop small muscles such as grasping, throwing, catching, rolling, squeezing, dropping, pounding, pulling, zipping, spreading, pouring, twisting, and buttoning.

- Planning and implementing increasingly difficult activities in which small muscles are used.

- Encouraging children to participate in daily routines such as setting the table for meals, wiping up spills, and sweeping sand.

Knowledge Assessment
Module 5: Cognitive

Multiple choice exercises. Select the best answer from those given.

1. Cognitive development is:

   a. _____ the growing ability to think and to reason.

   b. _____ related to other areas of development.

   c. _____ a lifelong process.

   d. _____ all of the above.

2. When a toddler calls a worm a "caterpillar," the child is:

   a. _____ making a mistake and should be told the right name.

   b. _____ noticing the ways in which a worm and a caterpillar are alike.

   c. _____ not very advanced in cognitive development.

   d. _____ obviously not ready to learn the difference between the two.

3. Which of the following prompts stretch children's thinking and problem-solving skills?

   a. _____ "What can we do to get that ball out from under the bush?"

   b. _____ "What will happen if we bring some snow inside?"

   c. _____ "Tell me about what you and your Grandma did last night."

   d. _____ "Can you count the toys that the baby in the picture is playing with?"

   e. _____ a and c.

   f. _____ all of the above.

4. Which of the following statements are **false**?

   a. _____ Providers should spend most of the day teaching children many facts.

   b. _____ Children develop social skills such as sharing and cooperating at the same time as they develop cognitive skills.

   c. _____ When providers help children see themselves as successful learners, it prepares them for school and life.

   d. _____ The best way to promote cognitive development is to teach children alphabet and number songs.

   e. _____ When children solve their own problems, they feel competent.

On the basis of knowledge gained through this module, complete the following exercises. Some require more than one answer. Partial credit will be given. Complete each exercise as thoroughly as you can.

5. What are infants learning when their providers play "peek-a-boo" with them?

   _____

   _____

   _____

6. Give **two** examples of how infants, toddlers, preschoolers, and school-age children learn.

   a. Infants:

   1. _____

   2. _____

   b. Toddlers:

   1. _____

   2. _____

   c. Preschoolers:

   1. _____

   2. _____

   d. School-age children:

   1. _____

   2. _____

7. Give **one** specific example of children using the following thinking skills.

   a. Noticing characteristics of things: _____

   _____

   _____

   b. Identifying likenesses and differences: _____

   _____

   _____

   c. Classifying: _____

   _____

   _____

d. Sequencing: _____

_____

_____

e. Understanding cause and effect: _____

_____

_____

f. Making predictions: _____

_____

_____

8. Why is it important to help children develop and use problem-solving skills?

_____

_____

_____

9. Give **two** examples of what providers can do to help infants use their senses to learn:

1. _____

_____

2. _____

_____

10. Give **two** examples of what providers can do to help toddlers develop cognitive skills:

1. _____

_____

2. _____

_____

11. Give **two** examples of what providers can do to help preschoolers develop cognitive skills:

1. _____

_____

2. _____

_____

12. Give **two** examples of what providers can do to help school-age children develop cognitive skills.

1. _____

   _____

2. _____

   _____

Competency Assessment
Module 5: Cognitive

During the observation period your trainer/mentor will assess whether you use skills such as the following:

- Using knowledge gained through observations to help individual children learn.

- Providing experiences and activities that allow children safely to use and refine their senses (touch, taste, hear, and smell).

- Talking with children about what they are doing, observing, learning, and feeling.

- Providing a variety of open-ended materials that can be explored and used in different ways by children of different ages.

- Providing toys, materials, and activities that challenge children and allow them to be successful.

- Providing opportunities for children to learn about similarities and differences, object permanence, cause and effect, and sequence.

- Asking open-ended questions and using other open-ended prompts that encourage children to think and express their ideas (for example, "I wonder what will happen when…").

- Respecting children's questions and responding in ways that promote thinking skills and more questioning.

- Providing assistance when children seem to need an adult's help.

- Allowing children to solve their own problems when they don't seem to need an adult's help.

- Using daily routines and household objects for learning.

- Providing materials and encouraging children to pursue projects and hobbies.

- Showing respect for and interest in children's ideas.

- Talking to children about what you and they are doing during daily routines (for example, "I see you have little goose bumps on your arms. I think you might be cold, so let's put your sweater on.").

Knowledge Assessment
Module 6: Communication

Matching exercise.

For each age group in the left column, find *three* characteristics in the right column that providers should look for when choosing books.

1. Infants   ____, ____, ____

     a.   have a lot of irony and humor

     b.   have clear, large illustrations

     c.   are imaginative stories with surprising or fantastic plots

2. Toddlers   ____, ____, ____

     d.   have lots of repetition and playful rhymes

     e.   are mysteries, adventure stories or fantasies

     f.   are small enough to handle

3. Preschoolers   ____, ____, ____

     g.   have plots about families, relationships, and school

     h.   are filled with pictures of familiar objects

     i.   are predictable and have lines that are repeated

4. School age   ____, ____, ____

     j.   extend their knowledge and understanding of the world

     k.   introduce beginning concepts such as push and pull or what grows in a garden

     l.   tell simple stories about people, things, and events familiar to them

Multiple choice exercise. Select the best answer from those given.

5. Learning to use verbal language as a way to communicate with others is important because:

     a. ____ it's the only way people communicate.

     b. ____ sense of self is affected by the ability to express feelings and thoughts verbally.

     c. ____ the sooner children learn to talk, the sooner they learn to read.

     d. ____ understanding and using language is important to cognitive development.

On the basis of knowledge gained through this module, complete the following exercises. Some require more than one answer. Partial credit will be given. Complete each exercise as thoroughly as you can.

6. What are **two** ways a provider can prepare the environment to support children's development of reading and writing skills?

    1. _____

    2. _____

7. Suggest **three** ways providers can use their own language skills to promote children's communication skills:

    1. _____

    _____

    2. _____

    _____

    3. _____

    _____

8. Describe how to read or share a book with a child in a specific age group.

    _____

    _____

    _____

9. What is meant by "accepting children's communication"?

    _____

    _____

    _____

10. What can a provider do to promote the communication skills of a child whose home language is different from hers?

    _____

    _____

    _____

121

11. When children are learning to communicate, they respond to language long before they say words. What are the next **five** stages of language development?

    1. _____

    2. _____

    3. _____

    4. _____

    5. _____

12. List one way a provider can encourage a child who does not talk very much.

    _____

    _____

    _____

Competency Assessment
Module 6: Communication

During the observation period your trainer/mentor will assess whether you use skills such as the following:

- Paying attention to children's nonverbal communication and helping them express their ideas and feelings (for example, "You look like you had a hard day at school. Would you like to talk about it?").

- Responding to infants' vocalizations—gurgling, cooing, crying, whimpering—by smiling and talking to them.

- Encouraging children to communicate with each other.

- Accepting children's way of speaking.

- Serving as a role model for using language.

- Conversing with children about their feelings, ideas, and activities.

- Listening attentively to what children say and respecting their ideas.

- Playing games, such as finger plays, that encourage children to talk and sing.

- Providing secure and inviting places for children to talk and play together.

- Providing props and supporting children's pretend and dramatic play.

- Providing books that are appropriate for children's ages and interests.

- Storing books attractively.

- Providing quiet, cozy places for looking at books and reading.

- Reading books with children every day.

- Providing a wide variety of paper and writing tools to encourage children to scribble and write.

- Modeling writing and reading as a part of daily activities.

- Using words and phrases from the children's home languages.

Knowledge Assessment
Module 7: Creative

On the basis of knowledge gained through this module, complete the following exercises. Some require more than one answer. Partial credit will be given. Complete each exercise as thoroughly as you can.

1. Creativity involves many characteristics, not just a particular skill or ability. Creativity involves _____

    _____

2. Ms. Gonzalez is feeding Teresita (10 months) yogurt and bananas. How can she use this routine to encourage creativity?

    _____

    _____

    _____

3. Bernard (4 yrs. old) likes digging in the sand and dirt. What are two ways his provider could encourage his creativity?

    _____

    _____

    _____

4. List **five** examples of materials that can be used for art experiences:

    1. _____   4. _____

    2. _____   5. _____

    3. _____

5. For each age group listed, describe how children might play with water.

    a. Infants: _____

    _____

    b. Toddlers: _____

    _____

    c. Preschoolers: _____

    _____

    d. School-age children: _____

    _____

6. Give **four** examples of props to use during sand play:

   1. _____   3. _____

   2. _____   4. _____

7. List **two** examples of how you think and express yourself creatively:

   1. _____

   _____

   2. _____

   _____

8. What are **two** ways a provider could offer opportunities for school-age children to explore art?

   1. _____

   2. _____

9. Describe an art activity/experience you have done (or would like to do) with the children in your care.

   _____

   _____

   _____

10. Children's drawing develops in several stages. Choose one stage and describe what children do at that stage. Describe how a provider can encourage the creativity of a child at that stage.

    Stage: _____

    _____

    _____

    What a provider can do: _____

    _____

    _____

11. Singing is an integral part of music and movement, and most children enjoy it. List **two** ways a provider can incorporate singing into everyday activities.

    1. _____

    _____

    2. _____

    _____

Matching exercise.

12. Match the characteristics of school-age children in the left column with the appropriate creative music and movement experience in the right column.

   a. ____ Developing leadership skills

   (1) Practicing the steps to the latest dances.

   b. ____ Curiosity about different things

   (2) Organizing the younger children for musical games.

   c. ____ Striving for competence

   (3) Choosing and taking care of records, tapes, and CDs on their own.

   d. ____ Involvement in entire process

   (4) Learning about different kinds of music and instruments.

   e. ____ Increasing independence

   (5) Participating in projects such as making homemade instruments by getting the materials, making something, and using it.

Multiple choice exercise. Select the best answer from those given.

13. Carlos (29 months) has been playing at the water table. He just poured water down the front of his shirt. Ms. Jones can encourage Carlos to continue exploring water by:

   a. _____ making sure he doesn't play there again until he can follow the rules.

   b. _____ calling his mother so she can come to pick him up.

   c. _____ telling him to get his dry clothes from his bin, helping him change, and gently reminding him of the rules about keeping the water in the table.

   d. _____ doing nothing so he can experience feeling wet.

Competency Assessment
Module 7: Creative

During the observation period your trainer/mentor will assess whether you use skills such as the following:

- Arranging the environment so that children can easily select, replace, and care for materials and equipment.

- Providing the space and time children need to explore, use their imaginations, make plans, and carry them out.

- Providing sufficient space for children's ongoing projects.

- Offering sensory experiences to stimulate children's imaginative and creative expression.

- Providing toys, materials, and activities that children can use in different ways (for example, blocks, sand and water play, plastic bowls and lids, a wagon).

- Providing dress-up clothes and props for pretend and dramatic play, and participating in children's play.

- Providing a variety of art materials that children can use for their own creations.

- Offering a variety of planned and spontaneous music and movement activities.

- Establishing a secure and trusting relationship with each child.

- Acknowledging children's creative thinking (for example, "I see that you opened both ends of the box. Now you can crawl through.").

- Supporting children to enable them to solve their own problems.

- Responding to younger children in ways that acknowledge their interest in the process of creating rather than the end product.

- Responding to older children in ways that acknowledge that they care about the products of their creative endeavors.

- Using open-ended questions and prompts that encourage creative thinking.

- Showing respect for children's creative effort by waiting until they are finished before asking them to do something else.

Knowledge Assessment
Module 8: Self

Multiple choice exercises. Select the best answer from those given.

1. A child's sense of self, which comes from daily experiences, develops:

    a. _____ from the time a child can speak and understand words and sentences.

    b. _____ from six months on.

    c. _____ from the time the child knows right from wrong.

    d. _____ from birth.

2. Repeating activities so that children can practice skills:

    a. _____ helps keep children as busy as possible for longer periods of the day.

    b. _____ helps children feel successful and competent.

    c. _____ is boring for a child and should not be done.

    d. _____ is boring for providers and should not be done.

3. Providers can build children's sense of self by:

    a. _____ showing respect for children and their families.

    b. _____ modeling an appreciation for all social groups.

    c. _____ expressing surprise and joy when children learn new things.

    d. _____ all of the above.

4. When a provider uses caring language throughout the day:

    a. _____ children learn that she cares about their well-being.

    b. _____ respect and concern for others is modeled.

    c. _____ she must listen to children to know how to respond.

    d. _____ it will become be a part of everyday communication.

    e. _____ all of the above.

On the basis of knowledge gained through this module, complete the following exercises. Some require more than one answer. Partial credit will be given. Complete each exercise as thoroughly as you can.

5. Rewrite these statements so they will promote children's positive sense of self.

    a. "Mary, you are getting on my nerves. I think you need a nap."

    _____

    _____

    _____

    b. "You are always spilling something. Go get a sponge from the sink so you can wipe up this mess."

    _____

    _____

    _____

    c. "Do you want to sit in the corner? Then leave Billy alone."

    _____

    _____

    _____

    d. "Every day you drop your books on the floor when you come back from school. Next time you do it, I'm throwing them away."

    _____

    _____

    _____

6. Define "positive sense of self."

    _____

    _____

    _____

7. List **three** things you do to enhance children's sense of self:

    1. _____

    2. _____

    3. _____

8. Why is it important for infants to develop a sense of trust?

    _____

    _____

9. What are **two** ways to help children handle separation?

    1. _____

    _____

    2. _____

    _____

10. Kevin (7 years old), is learning how to ride a two-wheeled bicycle. He can balance himself fairly well, but he has some trouble stopping and starting the bike. You're concerned that he will hurt himself if he can't stop right away, but he seems to enjoy trying to master this feat. How would you handle the situation?

    _____

    _____

    _____

11. Name **two** things you do to support your positive sense of self.

    1. _____

    2. _____

12. Match the following statements about children in the right column with the **approximate** age at which the behavior is typical.

    a. ___ 4 years   (1) Child is energetic and happy when parents are present and misses them when they are gone.

    b. ___ 2 months   (2) Child is used to being away from parents but may need extra support during new situations or long periods of separation.

    c. ___ 2 years   (3) Child may be terrified when parents are away.

    d. ___ 10 years   (4) Child knows parents will return and can usually handle separation during the day.

    e. ___ 16 months   (5) Child is not yet aware of being separate from his parents and will most likely not mind being with strangers.

Competency Assessment
Module 8: Self

During the observation period your trainer/mentor will assess whether you use skills such as the following:

- Planning the day's activities and providing materials that are appropriate for the children's needs, interests, and strengths.

- Displaying pictures of the children's families and providing space for personal belongings.

- Talking with children about their feelings so they can understand and express their emotions.

- Helping children make the transition from their homes to the FCC home.

- Giving individual attention to each child every day.

- Letting children know that you value them even when they have negative emotions or cannot control their behavior.

- Showing children in many ways that their well-being is important to you.

- Using verbal language and actions to express pleasure and interest in individual children and what they are doing.

- Helping children learn to express their ideas and feeling verbally.

- Modeling positive ways to talk and act to show other people that you care about them.

- Allowing and encouraging children to make choices.

- Offering appropriate help to children when they are learning new skills.

- Allowing children to learn from their mistakes and encouraging them to try a variety of problem-solving strategies.

- Repeating activities so children can practice and master skills.

- Providing appropriate levels of support so that children do as much as possible for themselves.

Knowledge Assessment
Module 9: Social

Multiple choice exercises. Select the best answer from those given.

1. Providers and other adults can best help children develop social skills by:

    a. _____ telling them what not to do.

    b. _____ letting children know they are loved and accepted.

    c. _____ correcting their mistakes as quickly as possible.

    d. _____ helping children learn to respect the rights of others.

2. Laura (10 months) grabs Dionne's (26 months) curly hair. Dionne screams. How might Ms. Lewis respond to help Laura learn about being with other people?

    a. _____ Pick up and comfort Dionne and ignore Laura.

    b. _____ Pick up Laura and put her in her crib. Tell her, "No. You can't do that to Dionne."

    c. _____ Comfort Dionne. Tell Laura, "It hurts when you pull Dionne's hair." Take Laura's hand and show her how to touch Dionne gently.

    d. _____ Tell Dionne to stay out of Laura's reach in the future.

On the basis of knowledge gained through this module, complete the following exercises. Some require more than one answer. Partial credit will be given. Complete each exercise as thoroughly as you can.

3. When children's needs are met consistently and promptly, children learn to trust other people and themselves. Why is this important for social development?

    _____

    _____

4. Describe **three** ways a provider can help children learn caring behaviors:

    1. _____

    2. _____

    3. _____

5. Playing simple games such as rolling a ball back and forth with an infant helps him learn _____, an important social skill.

6. List **three** examples of toys and materials that encourage children to play together:

    1. _____

    2. _____

    3. _____

7. Give an example of how children exhibit or begin to exhibit the following caring behaviors.

    a. Empathy: _____

    _____

    _____

    b. Generosity: _____

    _____

    _____

    c. Helping: _____

    _____

    _____

8. Give **two** examples of how providers can help a child who is shy, aggressive, or rejected?

    a. Shy child:

    1. _____

    2. _____

    b. Aggressive child:

    1. _____

    2. _____

    c. Rejected child:

    1. _____

    2. _____

9. Play is important to children's social development. Name **two** ways a provider can encourage and extend children's play.

    1. _____

    2. _____

10. List **two** ways a provider can arrange and organize the FCC home environment to make group living as comfortable as possible for everyone.

1. _____

_____

2. _____

_____

Matching exercise.

11. The column on the left lists examples of children's social behaviors. The column on the right lists the age group of which this behavior is typical. Match the appropriate age group with each social behavior.

a. ___ Young infants   (1) Andrea tightly holds her baby doll and says, "My baby."

b. ___ Mobile infants   (2) Chaundra tells her provider, "Tricia is my best friend, and she's going to spend the night at my house this weekend."

c. ___ Toddlers   (3) Mitzi crawls after Carl and Fred when they go into the living room.

d. ___ Preschoolers   (4) Victor says to Leon, "If you push me in the wagon then I'll push you next."

e. ___ School-age children   (5) Marvin starts to smile when his provider picks him up and rocks him.

Competency Assessment
Module 9: Social

During the observation period your trainer/mentor will assess whether you use skills such as the following:

- Observing and listening to learn how each child relates to the others in your care.

- Talking, making eye contact, and playing with children to give them experience in interacting with another person.

- Encouraging children to help each other.

- Supporting children to enable them to solve their own conflicts.

- Modeling positive ways to cooperate, share, and interact with others.

- Providing materials and activities that can involve two or more children at a time.

- Helping younger children express their feelings verbally and reminding older children to tell others how they feel.

- Providing a variety of props so children can use pretend and dramatic play to work through their fears and feelings.

- Expressing your own feelings when appropriate so children can learn to express their feelings.

- Verbally expressing what children may be feeling but are unable to express.

- Meeting young children's needs according to their personal schedules for eating, sleeping, and so on.

- Talking with children about what they are doing, to show your respect and appreciation for their efforts.

- Arranging the environment so children can be alone or with one or two others.

- Planning special group projects such as painting a mural so children of different ages can play and work together.

- Providing duplicates of favorite toys so children can play together without having to share before they are developmentally ready.

- Creating prop boxes with materials related to children's interests that can be used for pretend and dramatic play by children of different ages.

- Providing duplicates of certain dramatic play props, such as firefighter hats, to encourage group play.

- Providing some toys and materials, such as beads and string, that children may use when they want to play alone.

Knowledge Assessment
Module 10: Guidance

Multiple choice exercises. Select the best answer from those given.

1. People who are self-controlled can:

    a. _____ accept the results of their actions.

    b. _____ make independent choices.

    c. _____ balance their needs with those of others.

    d. _____ control their own behavior.

    e. _____ all of the above.

2. The most important goal of discipline is to:

    a. _____ keep children clean.

    b. _____ help children develop self-control.

    c. _____ maintain quiet.

    d. _____ get children to do what adults tell them.

3. Paul (32 months) is at the sand table. He keeps dumping handfuls of sand on the floor. Ms. Moore should:

    a. _____ tell Paul he can't play at the sand table any more.

    b. _____ remind Paul of the rules for the sand table and ask him to get the broom to sweep up the sand.

    c. _____ give Paul a warning about his behavior.

    d. _____ clean up the sand and make Paul sit by himself for 10 minutes.

4. Cassie (7 months) likes to grab Ms. Bates' eyeglasses. Which of the following is a developmentally appropriate way to help Cassie develop self-control?

    a. _____ Ms. Bates puts Cassie down and says, "No, " each time Cassie grabs the glasses.

    b. _____ Ms. Bates starts wearing contact lenses.

    c. _____ Ms. Bates gives Cassie an interesting item to hold before she picks her up.

    d. _____ Ms. Bates holds Cassie's hands and says, "No, leave my glasses alone."

    e. _____ Ms. Bates takes off her glasses and lets Cassie look through them.

On the basis of knowledge gained through this module, complete the following exercises. Some of them require more than one answer. Partial credit will be given. Complete each exercise as thoroughly as you can.

5. Rewrite the following statements so they provide positive guidance. There can be more than one correct answer.

   a. "Hurry up! All the other children have finished eating."

   _____

   _____

   _____

   b. "Get your stuff off the floor. Can't you see the little kids are trying to play?"

   _____

   _____

   _____

   c. "Big girls don't cry. You're old enough to know that you have to wait for your turn."

   _____

   _____

   _____

6. What is the difference between punishment and discipline?

   _____

   _____

   _____

7. Give **one** example of an appropriate way to provide discipline for each age group.

   a. Infants: _____

   _____

   b. Toddlers: _____

   _____

   c. Preschoolers: _____

   _____

   d. School-age children: _____

   _____

8. When one child bites another, how should a provider respond to the child who was hurt and to the child who did the biting?

   a. To the child who was hurt: _____

   _____

   _____

   b. To the child who did the biting: _____

   _____

   _____

9. List **one** rule for your FCC home. Then describe how you remind children of the rule when they forget.

   a. Rule: _____

   _____

   b. Reminder: _____

   _____

10. Tess (7 years) has told Donnie (4 1/2 years), "No! You can't play with me," several times this afternoon. Complete the following chart of what Ms. Moore can say to help Tess develop self-control:

Describe what happened:	
Tell the child what behavior is not acceptable:	
Tell the child what behavior is acceptable:	
Suggest a consequence for the behavior:	

Matching exercise.

11. The column on the left lists examples of children's behavior that may be affected by the environment. The column on the right lists changes in the environment that may address the problem behavior. Match the appropriate change in the environment with each behavior.

Children's Behavior		**Changes in the Environment**
a. _____ At clean-up time the children mix all of the toys together.	(1)	Make sure there is a specific area for quiet activities that is away from areas designated for more physical and noisy activities. Let the children know what each area is used for so that everyone can enjoy what they are doing.
b. _____ Children ask for help each time they want to play with a toy.	(2)	Assess the environment to make sure that the toys and materials meet children's needs and interests. Add new ones if needed. Talk with children to encourage their use of the materials and equipment outdoors.
c. _____ Children frequently argue about who will wear particular dress-up clothes.	(3)	Store toys in containers labeled with pictures or words.
d. _____ Children run around outside and rarely use the toys and equipment.	(4)	Provide plenty of dress-up clothes and duplicates of favorite items so that children can all find something they want to wear.
e. _____ Children who are reading are constantly interrupted by children who are running back and forth and bumping into them.	(5)	Display toys on low shelves where they can be reached by children.

Competency Assessment
Module 10: Guidance

Before the observation period your trainer/mentor will assess whether you use skills such as the following:

- Removing hazards so children can safely play and explore.

- Providing storage places with picture and word labels to show where things go.

- Keeping toys and other safe materials on low, open shelves so children can help themselves.

- Providing a place for older children to store their toys and materials out of the reach of the younger children.

- Providing a balanced, flexible daily schedule with time for both active and quiet play, indoors and outdoors.

During the observation period your trainer will assess whether you use skills such as the following:

- Providing a variety of materials and activities to meet children's needs, interests, and strengths.

- Providing sufficient developmentally appropriate materials, including duplicates of popular items.

- Involving children in setting limits and making rules.

- Trying to understand the possible reasons for children's behavior.

- Helping children to use problem-solving skills to resolve conflicts.

- Stating directions and reminding children of the rules in positive ways (e.g., "walk in the house").

- Reinforcing children's positive behavior with meaningful comments.

- Giving children opportunities to make developmentally appropriate choices.

- Modeling appropriate ways to express feelings.

- Providing soothing activities, such as playdough, water play, or simple crafts, and redirecting upset children to these activities.

- Talking to school-age children about their day at school, their friends, their concerns, and so on.

- Reminding children to use words to tell others how they feel.

- Working with families to help children express feelings in acceptable ways.

Knowledge Assessment
Module 11: Families

Multiple choice exercises. Select the best answer from those given.

1. Families and providers have the following in common:

   a. _____ they are child development experts.

   b. _____ they know exactly what the child needs.

   c. _____ they have genuine concern for the child's well-being.

   d. _____ they always know the reasons for the child's behavior.

2. When Mrs. Wright comes to pick up two-year-old Tanya, she asks the provider about Tanya's day. Which of the following is the most appropriate provider response?

   a. "Once she stopped fighting with Michelle, Tanya had a good time playing house."

   b. "Tanya had fun playing house with Michelle. They had a little trouble when they both wanted to use the same doll but solved their problem without my help."

   c. "Tanya must have gone to bed late last night. She was really mean today."

   d. "Tanya's day was fine."

On the basis of knowledge gained through this module, complete the following exercises. Some require more than one answer. Partial credit will be given. Complete each exercise as thoroughly as you can.

3. The most important people in a child's life are _____

4. Give **two** examples of things providers can do to maintain strong partnerships with families:

   1. _____

   _____

   2. _____

   _____

5. When a family asks for advice about allowing a 10-year-old more independence, how might a provider respond?

   _____

   _____

   _____

6. Give **two** examples of information about a child that is likely to be provided by a family and **two** provided by a provider:

   a. Family:

      1. _____

      2. _____

   b. Provider:

      1. _____

      2. _____

7. Families are interested in many kinds of information about their child's life at the FCC home. List **two** examples:

      1. _____

      2. _____

8. What are **two** things a provider can do to **plan** a successful family/provider conference?

      1. _____

      2. _____

9. What are **two** things a provider can do to **conduct** a successful family/provider conference?

      1. _____

      2. _____

10. State **one** way to involve family members who can't come to the FCC home during the day:

    _____

    _____

11. Describe **two** ways you support families:

    1. _____

    2. _____

12. Describe how you resolved a difference of opinion or a misunderstanding with a
    family. If you've never had a difference or a misunderstanding, describe a situation that
    might occur.

    _____

    _____

    _____

13. What are some sources of stress for families that providers should be aware of?

    _____

    _____

    _____

Competency Assessment
Module 11: Families

During the observation period (either at drop-off or pick-up time), your trainer/mentor will assess whether you use skills such as the following:

- Sharing with families information about their child's day—feedings or meal times, naps, play times and interactions.

- Helping families understand what their child learns through everyday activities.

- Sharing with families some good news about their child's day.

- Listening when families share information about their child.

- Involving families in making decisions about their child's care.

- Suggesting ways to support learning at home.

- Responding to families' questions and concerns about their child's development, as well as sharing their delight.

- Working with parents to plan strategies for handling behavior and responding to a child's readiness to learn.

- Sharing information with parents about current activities and future plans at the FCC home.

- Providing opportunities for families to be involved in the program.

- Helping families understand the stages of child development and the reasons for their child's behavior.

- Providing support for families under stress (if an opportunity arises during the observation period).

Knowledge Assessment
Module 12: Program Management

Multiple choice exercises. Select the best answer from those given.

1. Categories that can be used to organize your observation notes of children's development include:

    a. _____ language.

    b. _____ clothing.

    c. _____ fine and gross motor skills.

    d. _____ all of the above

    e. _____ a and c

2. Individualizing a program for children means:

    a. _____ spending 20 minutes a day working with each child on a one-to-one basis.

    b. _____ planning only activities in which every child can participate successfully.

    c. _____ using what you know about each child as you plan for each day.

    d. _____ planning activities based on things children don't do well.

On the basis of knowledge gained through this module, complete the following exercises. Some require more than one answer. Partial credit will be given. Complete each exercise as thoroughly as you can.

3. As they plan and conduct the FCC program, what should providers do to determine the program's effectiveness?

    _____

    _____

4. State **three** reasons why providers observe children:

    1. _____

    2. _____

    3. _____

5. Describe the system you use to observe children systematically:

    _____

    _____

    _____

6. What are the **two** most important things providers must keep in mind when recording children's behavior?

   1. _____

   2. _____

7. After a planned activity is completed, providers should take time to **evaluate** what happened. Explain why this is necessary.

   _____

   _____

8. Rewrite the following observation note so that it is objective:

   Germaine (11 months) was very aggressive again today. She crawled quickly over to Brett (12 months), grabbed the toy from his hand, and made him cry.

   _____

   _____

   _____

9. For each of the following categories, give **two** examples of what providers might include in their weekly plan.

   a. Changes to the environment:

   1. _____

   2. _____

   b. Special activity:

   1. _____

   2. _____

   c. Changes to daily routines:

   1. _____

   2. _____

   d. Family involvement:

   1. _____

   2. _____

   e. To do:

   1. _____

   2. _____

10. Describe your FCC home's policy and procedures for **two** of the following items:

    - Caring for sick children
    - Reporting children's injuries
    - Taking children on a neighborhood walk
    - Closing for bad weather
    - Guiding children's behavior

    1. _____

    _____

    _____

    _____

    2. _____

    _____

    _____

    _____

11. Describe how you organize and plan a typical day in your home. State at least **two** strategies you use to manage your program.

    1. _____

    _____

    2. _____

    _____

Knowledge Assessment
Module 13: Professionalism

Multiple choice exercises. Select the best answer from those given.

1. As defined in the module, a professional is someone who:

    a. _____ charges a fee for services.

    b. _____ went to college.

    c. _____ is certified by the state.

    d. _____ uses specialized knowledge or skills to do a job.

2. The benefits of maintaining a commitment to professionalism include:

    a. _____ building greater respect for the child care field.

    b. _____ helping children grow, develop, and learn.

    c. _____ supporting your competence.

    d. _____ all of the above.

3. Match the following descriptions of standards in the left column with the correct source in the left column.

    a. ____ An accreditation process for FCC homes that is conducted by the National Association for Family Child Care

    (1) Child Development Associate (CDA) Functional Areas

    b. ____ Descriptions of practices that are suitable for children at particular ages and stages of development

    (2) Family Child Care Accreditation Criteria (NAFCC)

    c. ____ Definition of 13 key skill areas needed by early childhood professionals

    (3) Developmentally Appropriate Practice

Multiple choice exercise. Select the best answer from those given.

4. Which of the following provider behaviors are ethical?

   a. _____ Taking a sick day when your mother comes to visit you.

   b. _____ Avoiding children you don't like.

   c. _____ Helping parents understand why their infant isn't walking yet.

   d. _____ Learning about another culture when a child from that culture joins your group.

   e. _____ Talking about a toddler's temper tantrum in front of another child's parents.

   f. _____ Maintaining accurate written records about each child.

   g. _____ Comforting a child who misses their parents.

   h. _____ Writing a letter to your Congressperson in support of child care legislation.

On the basis of knowledge gained through this module, complete the following exercises. Some require more than one answer. Partial credit will be given. Complete each exercise as thoroughly as you can.

5. List **two** strategies you use to continue learning about caring for children:

   1. _____

   _____

   2. _____

   _____

6. Explain why it is important to set goals for professional growth:

   _____

   _____

   _____

   _____

7. Give **two** examples of what you plan to do to contribute to child advocacy efforts:

   1. _____

   _____

   2. _____

   _____

8. Ms. Kim has been a provider for 10 years. What are **two** reasons why she needs to keep learning about child development and caregiving practices?

    1. _____

    2. _____

9. **Four** caregiving topics I want to learn more about are:

    1. _____

    2. _____

    3. _____

    4. _____

10. For each area listed below, give **one** example of something you did this week to take care of yourself.

    a. Physical well-being: _____

    _____

    b. Emotional well-being: _____

    _____

    c. Social well-being: _____

    _____

    d. Intellectual well-being: _____

    _____

11. Describe what being an early childhood professional means to you:

    _____

    _____

    _____

    _____

    _____

12. List **three** of the CDA functional areas that you enjoyed or look forward to working on:

    1. _____

    2. _____

    3. _____

Appendices

Appendix A

Planning Form for Group Sessions

Planning Form
for Group Sessions

Use this form to plan meetings of providers who are working on the same module. You may tailor the agenda to address special interests and individual training needs of providers.

Module: _____

Overview

A. Opening

Ask an open-ended question to promote a discussion of the topics addressed in this module.

_____

_____

_____

B. Discussion Questions

Be prepared to lead a discussion on the key points addressed in the module.

_____

_____

_____

_____

C. Review of Overview

1. Review the examples of strategies providers use in this functional area. Ask providers to give examples of how they use the strategies.

2. Discuss the vignettes, providers' responses to the questions, and the answers provided at the end of the module. Ask questions such as:

   • What do you think about the way the caregiver handled this situation?

   • How would you handle a similar situation in your home?

   _____

   _____

   _____

   _____

3. Discuss the section relating the providers' personal experiences to the topic of the module (e.g., Your Own Need for Safety).

Collect the pre-training assessments from providers and discuss their responses.

Learning Activity _____ *

A. Opening

Begin by asking an open-ended question, reviewing the previous learning activity, or discussing a follow-up assignment from the previous meeting.

_____

_____

_____

_____

B. Discussion Questions

Lead a discussion about the key points presented in the learning activity.

_____

_____

_____

_____

_____

_____

_____

_____

C. Review of Activity

Ask providers to describe their experiences completing this learning activity. Encourage them to share examples from their completed charts.

_____

_____

_____

_____

_____

_____

_____

_____

_____

_____

---

* Complete one planning form for each learning activity in this module.

D. Additional Resources/Activities

List here any materials, audiovisual resources, topics for discussion, or activities you will use to supplement the learning activities.

_____

_____

_____

_____

_____

E. Ending the Session

- Collect completed learning activity.

- Give a brief overview of the next learning activity.

_____

_____

_____

_____

_____

If this is the last session for the module, discuss Summarizing Your Progress.

- Have each person share one item from their summary of what they learned while working on this module.

- Ask providers to share some of the ways they adapted or changed their practices. How have children and families responded to the changes?

Then plan a time to meet individually with each provider and administer the assessments.

Appendix B

Answer Sheets for Knowledge Assessments

Module 1: Safe

Total of 100 points possible. Passing score is 80 or above.

Each Answer Worth	Possible Total Points	**Answer**
2 1/2	2 1/2	**1.** d
2 1/2	2 1/2	**2.** b
2 1/2	2 1/2	**3.** d
2 1/2	2 1/2	**4.** d
2 1/2	2 1/2	**5.** e
2 1/2	2 1/2	**6.** e

5 each   15

7. Examples of correct responses include the following:

- Children learn about safety from their providers and parents. For example, when a provider talks to children as she fastens safety straps on a highchair or stroller, or puts away a lamp with a frayed cord, the children learn about safety.

- Providers should develop evacuation procedures so they will know what to do if an actual emergency occurs. Well-thought-out plans will allow a provider to respond to an emergency quickly and calmly. Monthly fire drills help providers and children learn what to do in case an actual emergency does occur.

- It is extremely important for providers to consider the skills and abilities of the children in care when ensuring a safe environment. When a new child joins the group, a provider must assess the child's skills and abilities and determine whether the environment is safe for the new child. If necessary, the environment must be changed so that it is a safe place for the new child. This is especially critical if the new child has special needs.

5 ea.   10

8. Two responses are required. Any two items from the daily indoor safety checklist would be correct answers. If the provider gives answers that are not on the checklist, ask why checking these items will help maintain a safe indoor environment. If you agree that they would enhance safety, responses are correct.

5 ea.   10

9. Two responses are required. Any two items from the daily outdoor safety checklist would be correct answers. If the provider gives answers that are not on the checklist, ask why checking these items will help maintain a safe outdoor environment. If you agree that they would enhance safety, responses are correct.

5 ea.   10

10. One emergency situation and two responses are required, each worth 5 points. There are many potential emergency situations that a provider should be prepared for. Discuss with the provider why her answers would keep children safe. If you agree that they would enhance safety, consider the responses correct.

161

5 ea.	20	**11.** Four responses are required; one for each age group. There are many possible correct answers. The examples of what providers should do to keep children safe should be directly related to the examples of what children are like. Discuss answers with the provider to make sure she understands the relationship between child development and safe caregiving practices. Examples of correct responses include the following:

a. <u>Infants</u>:
Infants develop very quickly. They are curious and want to touch everything they see. This makes them very vulnerable to dangerous objects and safety hazards. Providers have to pay close attention to infants and make sure dangerous items such as electrical outlets, hanging items, cords, and sharp edges are not accessible.

b. <u>Toddlers</u>:
Toddlers are constantly on the move and like to explore things in their environment. Providers should explain the importance of safety to toddlers in simple language. Toddlers like to imitate adults and so providers should model safe behaviors as well as explain them.

c. <u>Preschoolers</u>:
Preschoolers like a lot of physical activity and are constantly jumping, hopping and exploring. Providers need to remind preschoolers of the safety rules and to make sure the indoor and outdoor FCC environment is clear of items and situations that would endanger the children. Preschoolers need a lot of room for gross motor activities, and providers should make sure they can practice their gross motor skills in an obstruction-free environment.

d. <u>School-age children</u>:
School-age children are interested in perfecting skills and may be tempted to try things that are too difficult. They want to be like their peers or older kids. Providers should supervise their physical activities and ensure that equipment they use is in good working condition and age appropriate. They should show school-age children the proper way to use equipment and potentially dangerous items. (See Activity III if you need more information.)

5 ea.	10	**12.** Two responses are required.

1. Do no harm.
2. Do not move a child with a serious head, neck, or back injury except to do CPR or otherwise save a life.

10	10	**13.** Provider's answer is based on personal experience. Any response which explains steps and precautions she took in an emergency is correct.

Module 2: Healthy

Total of 100 points possible. Passing score is 80 or above.

Each Answer Worth	Possible Total Points	**Answer**	
2 1/2	2 1/2	**1.**	d
2 1/2	2 1/2	**2.**	b
2 1/2	2 1/2	**3.**	c

2 1/2	2 1/2	**4.**	d.
5	5	**5.**	The following is an example of a correct response. Use judgment as to whether a provider's answer is acceptable.

5. Providers should place tissues and paper towels where children can reach them to encourage self-help skills. With assistance as needed, children can learn to help keep themselves healthy by wiping their own noses and washing their hands.

5 ea.	10	**6.**	Two responses are required. Examples of correct responses include the following:

- Provider must be trained by Preventive Medicine officials.
- Provider must have a completed and signed medication dispensation record provided by parent or guardian.
- Medication must be prescribed or otherwise authorized by the child's physician.
- Medication must be in original container labeled with child's name, dosage, and time to be dispensed.

10	10	**7.**	A safe disinfectant solution can be made by adding 1 tablespoon of bleach to a gallon of water, or 1 teaspoon of bleach to 1 quart of water.

5	5	**8.**	One response is required. Examples of correct responses include the following:

- Injuries to elbows, chins, noses, foreheads, and other bony areas.
- Bruises and marks on the soft tissue of the face, neck, buttocks, upper arms, thighs, ankles, backs of legs, or genitals.
- Swelling of the abdomen or head.
- Showing extreme concern when another child is crying.
- Showing no interest in other people; not crying or seeking attention.
- Crying, screaming, or refusing to go home with a parent or other caretaker.

5	5	**9.**	If a child's maltreatment is not reported, it is likely to continue.

5 ea.	15	**10.**	Three responses are required. Examples of correct responses include the following:

- Put disposable diapers in a plastic bag or plastic-lined container.
- Seal soiled cloth diapers in plastic bags and give to families to launder at home.
- Disinfect the changing table after each use.
- Wash children's hands after diapers are changed.
- Wash your own hands after completing the rest of the diapering procedure.
- Set up the changing area away from the eating area to prevent food contamination.

5 ea.	10	**11.**	Two responses are required. Possible correct responses include the following:

- Serve family-style meals so children can serve themselves.
- Plan and conduct simple food preparation activities.
- Serve as a model by tasting the food.
- Offer verbal encouragement.
- Offer a wide variety of finger foods so children can feed themselves.

5 ea.	10	**12.**	Two responses are required. Possible correct responses include the following:

- Decrease unnecessary stress in your life.
- Exercise more often.
- Quit smoking or do not start.
- Use relaxation techniques.

- Drink less alcohol.
- Eat foods low in salt, fats, and sugar.
- Get enough sleep each night.

5 ea.	10	**13.** Two responses are required. Any two items from the health checklist would be correct answers. If the provider gives answers that are not on the checklist, ask why the strategies will help maintain a healthy environment. Then make a judgment as to whether or not the responses are acceptable.
5 ea.	10	**14.** Two responses are required. Examples of correct responses include the following:

- Store materials and equipment for children's use in low cupboards or shelves.
- Place knives and other sharp items out of children's reach.
- Set up a child-sized table.
- Place the table near electrical outlets for appliances.
- Use an electric frying pan or wok instead of the stove.
- Provide duplicates of favorite utensils.
- Post kitchen safety signs.
- Keep only non-toxic cleaning supplies within children's reach.
- Lock up cleansers.
- Provide aprons or smocks.

Module 3: Learning Environment

Total of 100 points possible. Passing score is 80 or above.

Each Answer Worth	Possible Total Points	**Answer**
2 1/2	2 1/2	**1.** e
2 1/2	2 1/2	**2.** d
2 1/2	2 1/2	**3.** d
2 1/2	2 1/2	**4.** d
5 ea.	15	**5.** Two responses are required for each category. Possible correct responses include the following:

a. Indoor:
- Clearly define areas that are for children's play.
- Provide comfortable, cozy areas for children to sit, explore, read.
- Make toys and books accessible to children.
- Have a place for a child to work or be alone when she wants to be.
- Provide a variety of riding toys, equipment, and materials that are age-appropriate.
- Arrange the environment so children can practice self-help skills.

b. Outdoor:
- Organize outdoor areas so children can safely crawl, walk, climb, run, and play.
- Provide separate spaces outdoors for active and quiet play.
- Provide opportunities for outdoor games that encourage gross motor development (hopscotch, jump rope, playing ball, throwing frisbee).
- Take neighborhood walks to explore what is in the environment (trees, parks, changing seasons).

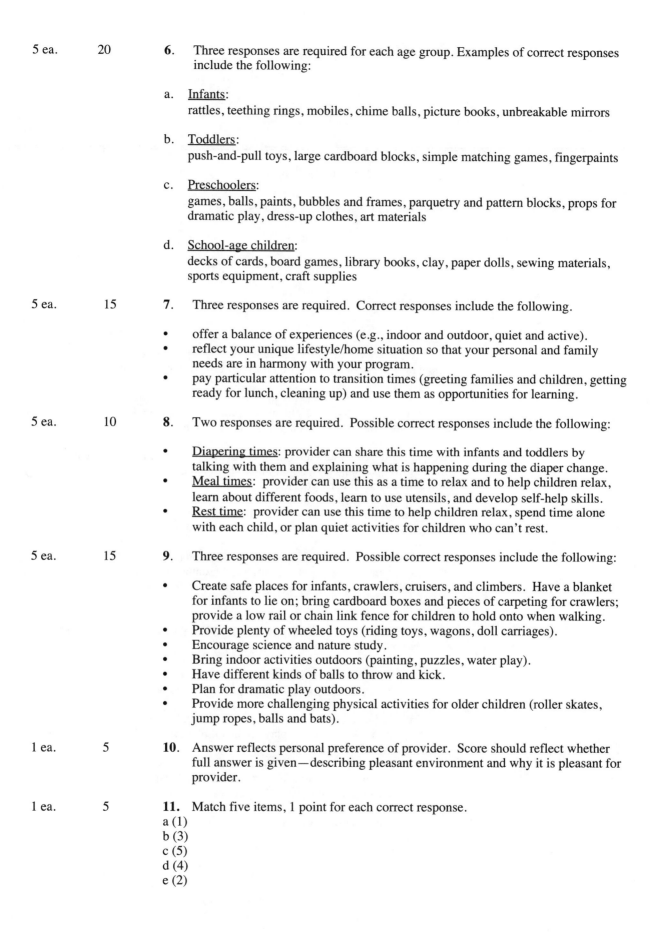

| 5 ea. | 20 | **6.** | Three responses are required for each age group. Examples of correct responses include the following: |

    a. <u>Infants</u>:
    rattles, teething rings, mobiles, chime balls, picture books, unbreakable mirrors

    b. <u>Toddlers</u>:
    push-and-pull toys, large cardboard blocks, simple matching games, fingerpaints

    c. <u>Preschoolers</u>:
    games, balls, paints, bubbles and frames, parquetry and pattern blocks, props for dramatic play, dress-up clothes, art materials

    d. <u>School-age children</u>:
    decks of cards, board games, library books, clay, paper dolls, sewing materials, sports equipment, craft supplies

| 5 ea. | 15 | **7.** | Three responses are required. Correct responses include the following. |

- offer a balance of experiences (e.g., indoor and outdoor, quiet and active).
- reflect your unique lifestyle/home situation so that your personal and family needs are in harmony with your program.
- pay particular attention to transition times (greeting families and children, getting ready for lunch, cleaning up) and use them as opportunities for learning.

| 5 ea. | 10 | **8.** | Two responses are required. Possible correct responses include the following: |

- <u>Diapering times</u>: provider can share this time with infants and toddlers by talking with them and explaining what is happening during the diaper change.
- <u>Meal times</u>: provider can use this as a time to relax and to help children relax, learn about different foods, learn to use utensils, and develop self-help skills.
- <u>Rest time</u>: provider can use this time to help children relax, spend time alone with each child, or plan quiet activities for children who can't rest.

| 5 ea. | 15 | **9.** | Three responses are required. Possible correct responses include the following: |

- Create safe places for infants, crawlers, cruisers, and climbers. Have a blanket for infants to lie on; bring cardboard boxes and pieces of carpeting for crawlers; provide a low rail or chain link fence for children to hold onto when walking.
- Provide plenty of wheeled toys (riding toys, wagons, doll carriages).
- Encourage science and nature study.
- Bring indoor activities outdoors (painting, puzzles, water play).
- Have different kinds of balls to throw and kick.
- Plan for dramatic play outdoors.
- Provide more challenging physical activities for older children (roller skates, jump ropes, balls and bats).

| 1 ea. | 5 | **10.** | Answer reflects personal preference of provider. Score should reflect whether full answer is given—describing pleasant environment and why it is pleasant for provider. |

| 1 ea. | 5 | **11.** | Match five items, 1 point for each correct response. |

a (1)
b (3)
c (5)
d (4)
e (2)

1 ea.	5	**12**. Match five items, 1 point for each correct response.

a (5)
b (4)
c (3)
d (1)
e (2)

Module 4: Physical

Total of 100 points possible. Passing score is 80 or above.

Each Answer Worth	Possible Total Points	**Answer**
2 1/2	2 1/2	**1.** e
2 1/2	2 1/2	**2.** e
5 ea.	10	**3.** Two responses are required. Sample correct responses such as the following show how to encourage children for their efforts, whatever their skill level:

- Review for children how to do an activity right before they try it. For example, "Chad (6 years), stand straight and tall, look straight ahead, and put one foot in front of the other as you walk along the balance beam."

- Respect children's individual differences and praise their progress without making comparisons to other children. For example: "Jettie (2 1/2 years), you came down the slide by yourself."

- Give verbal reassurance to a child who is frightened or reluctant. For example: "Hugo (3 years), I will hold your hand while you jump off the log."

- Give a child a suggestion of how to overcome an obstacle so he or she doesn't get too frustrated. For example: "Mariah (30 months), try using both hands to squeeze the water out of the sponge before you wipe the table. Then the table won't get too wet."

- Know when to stand back. For example: "Today I watched Jermaine (24 months) put his shoes on without any help."

- Encourage children to try new activities. For example: "Candyce (5 years) and Graham (4 1/2 years), would you like to carry the table outside?"

- Recognize when a child is not ready to try something. For example: "Isolina (32 months), if you don't want to play on the climber, that's okay. Maybe you would like to use the playdough."

- Acknowledge when a child tries something new. "Denise (8 years), I saw you dribbling the soccer ball today. Did you learn that at practice yesterday?"

| 5 | 5 | **4.** She might place an object a little out of reach to encourage the child to move to grasp the toy. |

5 ea.	10	**5.**	Two responses are required. Possible correct responses include the following:

a. Fine motor skills are movements using the small muscles of the body. Examples: picking up small items with thumb and forefinger, holding a paintbrush, using a spoon, putting pop beads together, taking a cover off a container, piling blocks, and turning the pages of a book.

b. Gross motor skills are movements using the large muscles of the entire body or large parts of the body. Examples: running, hopping, jumping, climbing, riding a bike, pulling a wagon, rolling over, crawling, getting in and out of a chair, kicking a ball, and pulling up to standing.

5 ea.	10	**6.**	Two responses are required. Examples of correct responses include the following:

- Holding a bottle or cup.
- Picking up small pieces of food with thumb and forefinger.
- Holding crackers or other finger foods.
- Holding a spoon and dipping it into food.
- Pouring juice.
- Wiping the table.
- Sweeping with a broom.
- Using a fork and other utensils.
- Carrying food to the table and dirty dishes away from the table.
- Passing plates and bowls to others.
- Folding napkins.
- Opening the door.
- Turning on water and washing hands.
- Tearing paper towel off the roll.
- Pulling up pants.
- Braiding hair.
- Tying shoelaces.

2 1/2 ea.	20	**7.**	Two responses are required for each activity. Possible total of 20 points for this question. Possible correct responses include the following:

a. Outdoor Play
- Walking to park.
- Running and jumping.
- Riding a bike or other wheeled toys.
- Playing ball.
- Climbing.

b. Blocks
- Lifting and moving blocks.
- Placing one block on top of another.
- Moving toy figures and vehicles far enough to require large body movements (e.g., reaching or crawling)
- Loading blocks in a wagon.

c. Music and Movement
- Swaying to music.
- Balancing in a rocking boat.
- Stepping up and down stairs on an upside-down rocking boat.
- Crawling in, out, and through a cardboard box.
- Walking along a balance beam or piece or rope.
- Making large movements in response to music.

d. Woodworking
- Making back-and-forth arm motions with saws and sandpaper.
- Making circular arm motions to use a hand drill.
- Carrying pieces of wood.

5   5   **8.** One response is required. Possible correct responses include the following:

- Getting some exercise is refreshing and helps the provider respond better to children's needs.
- The provider is showing the children that adults enjoy using their large muscles, too.

5 ea.   10   **9.** Two responses are required. Possible correct responses include the following:

- Bats and balls of different sizes.
- Tunnels or cardboard boxes to crawl through and in and out of.
- Climbers, slides, and swings.
- Rocking boats.
- Low balancing board.
- Bean bags to throw into containers.
- Items to help carry outdoors or in the room.
- Large hollow blocks.
- Cushions to jump on.
- Places and opportunities to run.
- Pull-toys to walk with.
- Music to move and dance to.
- Jump ropes.
- Bikes, wagons, doll carriages, and other wheeled toys.

5 ea.   10   **10.** Two responses are required. Examples of correct responses include the following:

- Simple puzzles.
- Painting at an easel.
- Fingerplays.
- Manipulatives such as large Legos, snap beads, or lacing boards.
- Containers and things to put in and take out of them.
- Meals served family-style so children can serve themselves.
- Looms and weaving materials.
- Knitting and crocheting supplies.

5 ea.   10   **11.** Two responses are required. Possible correct responses include the following:

- Keep lower back straight and avoid slouching when sitting or standing.
- Put one foot up on stool or step when standing for a long time.
- Bend knees, not back, when leaning forward.
- Wear low-heeled, comfortable shoes.
- Bend knees, tuck in buttocks, and pull in stomach muscles when lifting a child or heavy object.
- Avoid twisting when lifting or lowering a child or heavy object.
- Hold child or object close to body.
- Avoid standing for long periods of time with child on hip.
- Use a low chair with an adult-sized seat and backrest.
- Relax when possible; do some stretching exercises.

5	5	**12.** One response is required. Possible correct responses include the following:

- Watch what children are doing and encourage them as they learn and use physical skills.
- Use your knowledge of child development and of each child in care to know when to intervene directly and when to let children work out their own problems.
- Set clear limits with children so that they only do activities that are safe for them and others.
- Show children that movement and physical activities are enjoyable by participating with the children.
- Explain to children that physical activity and fitness are an important part of taking care of themselves.

Module 5: Cognitive

Total of 100 points possible. Passing score is 80 or above.

Each Answer Worth	Possible Total Points	**Answer**
2 1/2	2 1/2	**1.** d
2 1/2	2 1/2	**2.** b
2 1/2	5	**3.** f
2 1/2	5	**4.** a and d
5	5	**5.** Playing "peek-a-boo" helps infants begin to understand object permanence—an understanding that objects or people usually still exist even when they are out of sight. It also promotes turn taking
2 1/2 ea.	20	**6.** Two responses are required for each group. Possible correct responses include the following:

    a. <u>Infants</u>: learn by touching, tasting, moving, looking, playing, exploring.
    b. <u>Toddlers</u>: learn by handling objects, playing games, using blocks and other manipulatives, trying things over and over, moving.
    c. <u>Preschoolers</u>: learn by exploring, pretending, experimenting, creating.
    d. <u>School-age children</u>: learn by experimenting, focusing on meaningful projects/making things, playing games with rules, organizing and comparing, interacting with peers.

2 1/2 ea.	15	**7.** One response is required for each item. See Learning Activity III, Promoting Children's Thinking Skills, if you need more information. Examples of correct responses include the following:

    a. <u>Noticing characteristics of things</u>: Noting how something feels smells, looks, sounds, or tastes.
    b. <u>Identifying likenesses and differences</u>: Identifying how objects or living things are the same or not the same.
    c. <u>Classifying</u>: Grouping, matching, and sorting things and describing how and why they go together.
    d. <u>Sequencing</u>: Placing objects in order from large to small or dark to light; repeating a story in order of events or repeating a pattern.

e. <u>Understanding cause and effect</u>: Realizing that particular acts or conditions arise because of other acts or conditions.

f. <u>Making predictions</u>: Imagining what will happen if something else happens, or what will happen next or in the future.

| 5 | 5 |

8. The following is a sample correct response:

Children can use problem-solving skills to make sense of the world. Solving problems also helps children to develop a positive sense of self. When they learn to solve their own problems, children feel confident about their abilities.

| 5 ea. | 10 |

9. Two responses are required. Possible correct responses include the following:

- Provide safe, soft, washable, colorful toys to look at, shake, and mouth.
- Talk with infants and respond to their vocalizations and gaze.
- Give infants many opportunities to study the faces of providers and other children.
- Hang interesting things where infants can see and touch them.
- Give infants finger foods they can handle and eat.
- Talk about how different items smell.
- Arrange the environment so infants can explore safely.

| 5 ea. | 10 |

10. Two responses are required. Possible correct responses include the following:

- Extend toddler's statements. For example, if a toddler says, "Cup," the provider could say, "Yes, that's a tall, red cup."
- Provide toddlers with lots of room to move and explore.
- Allow toddlers time to finish what they are doing.
- Store toys and material on low, open shelves where toddlers can reach them.

| 5 ea. | 10 |

11. Two responses are required. Possible correct responses include the following:

- Talk to children about what they are doing, thinking, and feeling.
- Ask questions that help children think about problems and encourage them to come up with solutions. For example, "That's a great bridge you've built with the blocks and Legos. Do you think it's possible for two cars to go across it at the same time?"
- Provide materials and opportunities for children to role play and talk to them about what they are doing. For example, "You are a very careful doctor. What tools are you using for the operation?"

| 5 ea. | 10 |

12. Two responses are required. Possible correct responses include the following:

- Have children write poems or make up short stories.
- Encourage children to do long-term projects, such as a science or craft project.
- Ask children to think about and express their opinions on current issues in their community or school. Ask how these issues affect everyone.
- Provide children with a variety of reading materials (newspapers, magazines, books) and have them write their own articles, including book or movie reviews.
- Provide board games and puzzles that challenge and interest this age group.

Module 6: Communication

Total of 100 points possible. Passing score is 80 or above.

Each Answer Worth	Possible Total Points	**Answer**
2 1/2 ea.	7.5	**1.** b, f, h
2 1/2 ea.	7.5	**2.** i, k, l
2 1/2 ea.	7.5	**3.** c, d, j
2 1/2 ea.	7.5	**4.** a, e, g
2 1/2 ea.	5	**5.** b and d

5 ea.   10   **6.** Two responses are required. Possible correct responses include the following:

- Make signs, labels, charts, and lists and post them in the FCC home.
- Provide dramatic play props such as magazines, books, markers, tape, and construction paper that encourage literacy.
- Provide a variety of books that match the children's developmental levels and display them attractively.
- Record group stories, such as stories about walks, activities, or a visit from the mail carrier.

5 ea.   15   **7.** Three responses are required. Examples of correct responses include the following:

- Talk often, using a normal tone of voice and conventional vocabulary.
- Talk to children about what they are doing, and name things for them.
- Use interesting words even though children may not be able to say them, for example, "spaghetti," "somersault," or "petunia."
- Talk with children about their feelings.
- Make up rhymes and silly words.
- Use songs and finger plays.
- Display pictures and talk to children about what they notice the pictures.
- Read books and point to pictures. Talk about what they represent.
- Be quiet sometimes, in order to listen to what children are saying.

10   10   **8.** One response is required. Examples of correct responses include the following:

Infants:
- Spend one-on-one time with an infant, looking at a book or other reading material together. Remember, the goal is to share the experience rather than get through the book.
- Talk to infant as you look at the pictures. For example: "See the big dog."
- Point to pictures and ask simple questions. For example: "Do you know what that is?" Then model the answer.
- Let the infant touch the pages and handle the book.

Toddlers:
- Repeat phrases from the book.
- Pause during reading to allow the toddler to predict or repeat a phrase or word.

- Show or point to words as you read.
- Let the toddler read to you. It probably won't be word for word, but it lets the toddler practice recalling and telling the story.

Preschoolers:
- Tie the theme of the book to a recent experience of the preschooler.
- Hold the book at the child's eye level.
- Speak in a clear voice, with varied tones to suit the story.
- Ask questions to get the child involved and to keep his attention.

School-age children:
- Take cues from the child about when to share reading, instead of having planned reading times. If the child seems to need help choosing a book or is having difficulty reading, give individual attention.
- Share a book by reading a chapter or two together. Then discuss your impressions and ask open-ended questions about the content.
- Let beginning readers read to you. Be patient as they figure out the text.
- After reading a book, have the child or children put on a play about the story.

10   10   **9.** Accepting children's communication means appreciating the language skills the children have and modeling language instead of correcting children's grammar or pronunciation. For example if a child says "I don't got none," you would say, "You don't have any? Well, let's get you one." It also means being aware of and sensitive to the fact that there are various dialects and that no one dialect is better than another.

10   10   **10.** Ask the child's family for assistance in learning key words and phrases in their home language. Use the phrases when expressing yourself to the child and to find out what the child is trying to communicate. Follow regular routines so the child will feel comfortable and be confident that she knows what to do and when to do it. Make your home a place where an English language learner may take a break from the pressures of communicating verbally and observe until she is ready to join. Keep your language simple and combine nonverbal communication (gestures, intonation, gaze, and facial expressions) with your speech. Stress and repeat important words. Speak clearly and give the child plenty of time to express herself. Describe what you and the child are seeing and doing. Offer predictable books that encourage the child to join the reading by repeating key phrases. Invite the family to donate play props that include their home language (e.g., empty food containers, calendars, and menus).

1   5   **11.** Five responses are required. Vocalization, Word Development, Sentences, Elaboration, and Graphic Representation.

5   5   **12.** One response is required. Examples of correct responses include the following:

- Ask open-ended questions and offer open-ended prompts that require children to respond with more than just "yes" or "no".
- Talk to the child about how things feel, smell, taste, sound, and look.
- Spend time with children so they feel comfortable talking with you.
- Allow children to record themselves telling a story and play it back for them.
- Encourage conversation at mealtimes.
- Encourage children to talk about their feelings. Model words to label feelings.

Module 7: Creative

Total of 100 points possible. Passing score is 80 or above.

Each Answer Worth	Possible Total Points	**Answer**
2 1/2	2 1/2	**1.** There are several possible correct responses. A response is correct if it shows the provider's understanding that creativity involves new ways of doing things, trying ideas for new purposes, curiosity, taking risks, and learning from mistakes.
5	5	**2.** Any responses that show the provider's understanding of how infants use their senses to explore would be correct. Correct responses should include some or all of the following points:

     • Ms. Gonzalez might give Teresita her own spoon so she can explore the utensil.
     • She can talk to Teresita about how the yogurt and bananas taste, smell, feel, and look.
     • She can cut up some of the banana in pieces so Teresita can pick up the pieces with her hands and directly experience how they feel.
     • She can make up a song about bananas or about how much Teresita likes yogurt and bananas.

| 5 | 5 | **3.** One response is required. Examples of correct responses include the following: |

     • Make sand and water activities a regular part of the program.
     • Provide props such as a shovel and pail.
     • Encourage him to experiment by adding water to the sand.
     • Talk with him about what he is doing when he is playing with sand and water.
     • Encourage him to try different props for pouring and sifting sand.

| 1 ea. | 5 | **4.** Five responses are required. See module for listings of different types of materials. Examples of correct responses include the following: |

     • Brushes, paints.
     • Clay and playdough.
     • Crayons and drawing materials.
     • Sewing items and fabrics; yarn.
     • Scraps of building materials.
     • Paste or glue.
     • Scissors.
     • Stones, pebbles, flowers, seashells.
     • Household items—bottle tops, popsicle sticks, string, egg cartons.
     • Eggshells.
     • Straws.

| 5 ea. | 20 | **5.** Four responses are required. Possible correct responses include the following: |

    a. <u>Infants</u>: can sit on a towel on the floor and play with water in a basin placed in front of them. It is best to have a separate tub for each infant.
    b. <u>Toddlers</u>: can stand at a water table or on a low stool. They will enjoy playing with two or three other children and using a variety of props.
    c. <u>Preschoolers</u>: can experiment with pouring water on different surfaces or using different objects in the water. They can experiment and learn about measurement, sinking and floating, water absorption, evaporation, and other properties of materials.

d. <u>School-age children</u>: can make elaborate water works or add sand. They might lead younger children in a project. They can plan and conduct experiments using sand, water, and other materials.

2 1/2 ea.   10   **6.** Four responses are required. See the module for listings of props. Examples of correct responses include the following:

• Muffin tins	• Whisk brooms	• Small plastic vehicles
• Scoops	• Shovels	• Measuring cups
• Magnifying glass	• Gelatin mold	• Funnels
• Scale	• Rolling pin	• Animal and people figures

5 ea.   10   **7.** Two responses are required. Responses will vary according to the experiences of the providers. Use your own judgment to assess whether to consider a response correct.

5 ea.   10   **8.** Two responses are required. Possible correct responses include the following:

- Provide or encourage craft projects children can complete by themselves.
- Provide opportunities to learn skills such as knitting, weaving, or tie-dying.
- Have older children do art activities with the younger ones. They can help set up or clean up or lead the children during the activity.
- Provide and display various kinds of materials children can try on their own.

10   10   **9.** Response will depend on individual provider's experience. Judge whether the activity encouraged creativity. Keep in mind the types of materials used (no pre-cut shapes, coloring books, or close-ended materials).

5 ea.   10   **10.** Two responses are required. Consult module for chart on developmental stages of children's drawing (Learning Activity III). For first part, provider describes basic characteristics of one stage. For second part, provider gives ways to encourage creativity of a child at that stage. Give partial credit if only one part is addressed.

2 1/2 ea.   5   **11.** Two responses are required. There are many correct responses. Possible responses include the following:

- Transition times—beginning/end of day, lunch break, changing activities.
- Story time.
- During games.
- Have children make up songs—make a game of it.
- Have children record songs.

1 ea.   5   **12.** Match five items, 1 point for each correct response.
a (2)
b (4)
c (1)
d (5)
e (3)

2 1/2   2 1/2   **13.** c

174

Module 8: Self

Total of 100 points possible. Passing score is 80 or above.

Each Answer Worth	Possible Total Points	**Answer**	
2 1/2	2 1/2	**1.**	d
2 1/2	2 1/2	**2.**	b
2 1/2	2 1/2	**3.**	d
2 1/2	2 1/2	**4.**	e

5 ea.   20   **5.**   Four responses are required. The following are examples of correct responses. Use your own judgment to determine whether a provider's responses show that she understands how to use caring language.

    a.   "Mary, I think you are tired. I will help you get to sleep."

    b.   "Everyone has accidents. Don't worry. Get a sponge from the sink so you can wipe up the juice."

    c.   "Billy doesn't like it when you bother him. It makes him feel angry. I'll help you find something else to do."

    d.   "I think you need a place to put your books when you come in from school. How about putting them on the dining room table, where they'll be safe until it's time to go home?"

10   10   **6.**   A well-thought-out definition will include some of the following points:

- Sense of one's own worth.
- Confidence about who one is and what one can do.
- Feeling connected to others.
- Feeling respected and valued by others.
- Feeling competent (able to do things).

5 ea.   15   **7.**   Three responses are required. Any three appropriate responses are acceptable.

10   10   **8.**   Correct responses should include the following information:

An infant's sense of trust is the beginning of a sense of self. When infants' needs are not met promptly, consistently, and with love, it is very difficult for them to learn to trust. Infants do not venture out into the world unless they are assured that the world is a place where their needs will be met.

5 ea.   10   **9.**   Two responses are required. Examples of correct responses include the following:

- Encourage families to spend time in the FCC home so the child will feel more secure.
- Help families say goodbye; don't let them sneak out.
- Help children express and manage their feelings.
- Include items from children's homes.
- Talk with children about their families during the day.

- Involve younger children in games that help them understand and master separation (hide-and-seek, peek-a-boo, etc.).
- Encourage families to make a ritual out of saying goodbye.

10	10	**10.**	The following is a sample correct response. Use your judgment to determine whether provider's response considers the age, ability, and safety of the child.

Because Kevin enjoys trying to master bike riding and is not frustrated by his lack of complete control over the bike, I would not prevent him from trying to ride. However, I would set limits on where he may ride so that he would be safe if he could not stop quickly or if he fell off. I would even offer some tips on ways to stop safely and how to balance more quickly when starting off.

5 ea.	10	**11.**	Responses are innumerable, of course. Provider should name at least **two** things she does that give her a positive sense of self.

1 ea.	5	**12.**	Match five items, 1 point for each correct response.

a (2)
b (5)
c (1)
d (4)
e (3)

Module 9: Social

Total of 100 points possible. Passing score is 80 or above.

Each Answer Worth	Possible Total Points	**Answer**	
2 1/2	2 1/2	**1.**	b and d
2 1/2	2 1/2	**2.**	c
5	5	**3.**	When children trust themselves and others, they feel secure enough to explore the world and interact with other people.
5 ea.	15	**4.**	Three responses are required. Use your own judgment to determine whether a provider's responses show an understanding of how to help children learn caring behaviors. The following are examples of correct responses.

- Responding to children's cries of distress promptly and consistently.
- Developing a loving and nurturing relationship with each child.
- Encouraging and acknowledging cooperation and thoughtfulness.
- Planning group activities that involve collaboration and a sense of community.
- Modeling caring behaviors—sharing, showing concern or delight for another person, helping.
- Helping children learn that feelings can be labeled and expressed verbally.
- Providing many opportunities for children to play with one another.
- Coaching children's interactions with each other.
- Using each child's name often—label personal items, sing songs with names, talk to children about each other using names, use children's names during interactions.
- Asking children to help the provider or another child to do something meaningful.
- Showing respect for children as human beings.
- Giving children cooperative play ideas.

176

| 5 | 5 | **5.** One response is required. Examples of correct responses include the following: |

- To take turns.
- To initiate a game.
- To interact with another person.

| 5 ea. | 15 | **6.** Three responses are required. Examples of correct responses include the following: |

- A rocking boat.
- A two-sided easel.
- Jump ropes.
- Dramatic and pretend play props.
- Water and sand play.
- Sports equipment.
- Board games.
- A tunnel.
- Musical games (musical chairs, hokey pokey).
- Bins or baskets filled with a large number of blocks or pop beads.

| 5 ea. | 15 | **7.** Three responses are required, one for each caring behavior. Examples of the types of responses that would be appropriate include the following: |

a. Empathy:
- Astrid (34 months) jumps up and down with Kisha (3 years) when Kisha's mother comes to pick her up.

- Marty (38 months) says, "You okay?" to the provider when she bumps her knee.

b. Generosity:
- Tariq (36 months) offers one of his apple slices to his provider.

- Mia (5 years) lets one of the infants hold her favorite doll.

c. Helping:
- Zara (8 years) helps Shannon (2 years) tie her shoes.

- Dylan (6 years) picks up the rattle Ursula (4 months) drops on the floor.

| 2 1/2 | 15 | **8.** Three responses are required, two for each type of behavior. Examples of correct responses include the following: |

a. Shy child:
- Establish a warm and nurturing connection with the child.
- Observe to see how the child plays and interacts with others, what child likes to do, and what skills the child has.
- Use the information gathered through observation to talk with child about things he/she likes to do.
- Plan situations or activities that the child likes.
- Reassure the child that it is okay to play alone if he/she wants, but also coach the child about how to play and talk with the other children.
- Encourage some of the more socially competent children to involve the shy child in an activity.

b. Aggressive child:
- Redirect child's behavior.
- Encourage physical activities that the child enjoys to channel aggressive energy.

- Observe the child to see how he/she interacts with others and what triggers the aggression.
- Spend time alone with child to build a nurturing and trusting relationship.
- Help the child develop ways to achieve goals without being aggressive.
- Use child's positive characteristics to help others accept him/her as part of the group.

c. Rejected child:
- Coach the child on how to join in activities.
- Encourage child to discuss his or her feelings about being rejected. See if child understands the nature of the problem.
- Help all children understand acceptable behavior and ways children should interact with each other.
- Observe child to see why he or she has trouble joining or staying involved in an activity. Note any inappropriate behavior and help child learn more appropriate ways to behave.

5 ea.	10	**9.**	Two responses are required. Examples of correct responses include the following:

- Providing children with enough space, materials, and time for play.
- Modeling play behaviors.
- Reinforcing prosocial behaviors when they are observed.
- Helping children get started with play, but learning when to step back.
- Referring to children by their role names during dramatic and pretend play.
- Including and encouraging older children to be a part of younger children's play.

5 ea.	10	**10.**	Two responses are required. Possible correct responses include the following:

- Providing spaces for each child to store personal belongings.
- Having duplicates of popular materials and toys.
- Displaying pictures and other items from children's homes.
- Providing concrete ways to let children know when their turn will come or when it's the end of an activity.
- Helping children solve social problems; encouraging interaction among children of different ages.

1 ea.	5	**11.**	Match five items (1 point for each correct response).

a (5)
b (3)
c (1)
d (4)
e (2)

Module 10: Guidance

Total of 100 points possible. Passing score is 80 or above.

Each Answer Worth	Possible Total Points		**Answer**
2 1/2	2 1/2	**1.**	e
2 1/2	2 1/2	**2.**	b
2 1/2	2 1/2	**3.**	b

2 1/2	2 1/2	**4.**	c

<table>
<tr><td>5 ea.</td><td>15</td><td>**5.**</td><td>Three responses are required. The following are examples of correct responses. Correct responses should show that the provider understands how to use words to provide positive guidance.</td></tr>
</table>

    a.   <u>"Hurry up!"</u>

- "Do you need a little more time to finish your lunch, Bernie? You may take a few more minutes. Then it will be time to get ready for your nap."

- "Do you feel okay, Bernie? You usually eat more at lunch time. If you are finished, you may clear these dishes and get ready for your nap."

- "You look like you have had enough to eat, Bernie. Now it's time to clear the dishes and get ready for your nap."

    b.   <u>"Get your stuff off the floor."</u>
- "Nadine, I think it might be easier for you to work on your project at the table. Would you like some help moving your things?"

- "Nadine, we'll all help you move your things to the table. Then you'll have room to work, and the little kids won't get in your way."

- "Nadine, it seems like the little kids are going to be in your way. If you work at the table and they play on the floor, you won't be in each other's way."

    c.   <u>"Big girls don't cry!"</u>
- "I know it's hard to wait when you really want to do something. When Rita is finished with the Big Wheel you may have your turn."

- "You may have your turn on the Big Wheel when Rita is finished. Would you like a ride in the wagon while you are waiting?"

- "Ask Rita to tell you when she is finished riding the Big Wheel. You may play in the sand box or play catch with me until then."

5 ea.	10	**6.**	Punishment means controlling children's behavior through fear. Discipline means positively guiding and directing children toward acceptable behavior.

5 ea.	20	**7.**	There are four parts to this question. Examples of correct responses include the following:

    a.   <u>Infants</u>:
- Keep infants away from potential problems.
- Organize daily routines so that infants do not have to wait long to have their needs met.
- Use "no" sparingly. Save it for dangerous situations.
- Remove unsafe objects and situations from the environment.
- Offer another item if the one the child wants is unsafe for his level of development or being used by someone else.
- Separate children who are hurting each other.
- If nobody will be hurt, give infants a chance to solve their own problems but be available to help if necessary.

    b.   <u>Toddlers</u> (Many of the above suggestions are appropriate for toddlers as well as infants):
- Make positive suggestions, for example, "Let's set the table for lunch."

- Provide opportunities for toddlers to practice saying "no."
- Encourage toddlers to participate in daily routines so they can feel competent.
- Provide duplicates of popular toys.
- Store toys and equipment on low shelves.
- Use simple, positive reminders of rules and limits.
- Model acceptable ways to express feelings.
- Let children know that you understand how they are feeling.
- Try to understand the reasons for children's behavior.
- Tell children what they may do rather than what they may not do.

c. Preschoolers (Many of the above suggestions are appropriate for preschoolers as well as infants and toddlers):
- Recognize when children are restless and suggest more physically active activities.
- Involve children in making rules so they can make decisions and understand why rules are important.
- Set up a system for taking turns with popular toys or activities.
- Invite children to help you so they feel competent.
- Hold an out-of-control child until he or she regains control.

d. School-age children (Many of the above suggestions are appropriate for school-age children as well as infants, toddlers, and preschoolers):
- Plan your daily schedule so that you have time to pay attention to the school-age children, especially when they arrive after school.
- Provide a quiet place for children to do their homework if they choose.
- Ask children about their interests and what kinds of materials and activities they would like in the FCC home.
- Allow children to select their own materials and activities from what is available.
- Give school-age children a safe place to store their belongings and their projects.
- Encourage school-age children to be involved with the younger children by playing with them, reading to them, teaching them how to do things, and so on.

5 ea.   10   **8.** Two responses are required. Possible correct responses include the following:

a. To the child who was hurt:
- Comfort the child and wash the wound (offer a piece of ice to reduce the pain and swelling).

- Help the child to express his pain and feelings about being bit. Reassure the child that it isn't acceptable to hurt others or have other people hurt her or him.

b. To the child who did the biting:
- Tell the child that you will not allow her or him to bite another child. Explain that the other child doesn't like it because it hurts. Ask the child who did the biting to help you care for the bitten child.

- Try to find out why the child bit. Watch the child closely in the future and step in to prevent future biting incidents.

5 ea.   10   **9.** Two responses are required: one rule and a description of a reminder. The rule listed will depend on the ages of the children in care. Use your own judgment to determine if a provider's responses show that she understands how to establish rules and help children remember to follow them.

5 ea.   20   **10.** Four responses are required. An example of a correct response follows.

Describe what happened: Tess, several times this afternoon you hurt Donnie's feelings by the way you spoke to him.

Tell the child what behavior is not acceptable: I won't let you speak to other children in ways that make them feel badly about themselves or hurt their feelings.

Tell the child what behavior is acceptable: You may tell Donnie politely that you would like to play alone today.

Explain a consequence for the behavior: Donnie will feel better if you explain that you are still his friend even though you sometimes want to play alone.

1 ea.	5	**11.** Match five items, 1 point for each correct response. a (3) b (5) c (4) d (2) e (1)

Module 11: Families

Total of 100 points possible. Passing score is 80 or above.

Each Answer Worth	Possible Total Points	**Answer**
2 1/2	2 1/2	**1.** c
2 1/2	2 1/2	**2.** b
5	5	**3.** Possible correct responses include: parents, the family, guardian, or whoever is the primary person in a child's home life.
5 ea.	10	**4.** Two responses are required. Examples of correct responses include the following: • Communicate as often as possible with families by any effective means: notes, newsletters, telephone, during drop-off and pickup. • Talk to families about their concerns, even if the concerns seem unimportant. • When families make suggestions related to their children's care, do what they suggest or explain why you are not following them and try to resolve the difference. • Tell parents about their child's accomplishments without comparing the child to others. • Wait until you are asked before offering advice. • Tell families about the positive things that involve their children each day. • Acknowledge events and transitions in the families' lives.
5	5	**5.** The provider's response should demonstrate that she understands the importance of helping families discover what works best for them and their child. It is not always appropriate for providers to assume the role of a child development expert. It is more important to help families realize how competent they are and what good ideas they have for supporting their child's development and learning.

5 ea.	20	**6.** Two responses are required for each source. Examples of correct responses include the following:

a. <u>Family:</u>
- Health and growth history
- Favorite foods
- Food allergies
- The child's fears
- The family's preferences for care

b. <u>Provider:</u>
- Favorite play materials
- How the child plays with others
- What the child does when family members leave
- Which toys are frustrating
- What challenges the child enjoys

For additional correct responses, refer to Learning Activity II, Working Together to Support Children.

5 ea.	10	**7.** Two responses are required. There are many correct responses. Use your own judgment to determine if the provider's responses are correct. Examples of correct responses include the following:

- How the provider interacts with the child.
- What the child does during the day.
- New skills the child has learned.
- Any problems.
- What's on the menu this week.
- What new materials and equipment are available at the FCC home.
- Who has been sick and what they had.
- With whom the child plays.

5 ea.	10	**8.** Two responses are required. Examples of correct responses include the following:

- Let families know the purpose of the conference and ask them to share their goals for the conference.
- Review observation notes.
- Review anecdotal records.
- Collect samples of child's work (e.g., drawings, projects).
- Role-play with a colleague.
- Complete a planning form.

For additional correct responses, refer to Learning Activity IV, Planning and Participating in Conferences With Families.

5 ea.	10	**9.** Two responses are required. Possible correct responses include the following:

- Try to establish a relaxed tone.
- Begin and end with a positive statement about her relationship with the child.
- Ask families open-ended questions.
- Listen to families in order to respond.
- Answer families' questions or explain that you will try to find out the answers.
- Provide examples of the child's development and learning.
- Summarize the discussion at the end.

For additional correct responses, refer to Learning Activity IV, Planning and Participating in Conferences With Families.

5	5	**10.** One response is required. There are many correct responses. Use your own judgment to determine if the provider's responses are correct. Examples of correct responses include the following:

- Mending torn books or repairing broken toys
- Helping plant a garden on the weekend
- Helping build a new climbing structure for the yard (on weekends)
- Recording tapes of books or songs
- Making curtains for a puppet theater
- Making toys for the FCC home (provider can provide instructions)
- Collecting materials provider can use to make toys or storage areas

5 ea.	10	**11.** Two responses are required. Answers will depend on the provider, the children in her care, and the parents. Generally, responses should address helping parents find resources in the community or giving information and guidance on child growth and development. If answers indicate that the provider is assuming too much responsibility for supporting a family, discuss with her when to provide support and when to refer parents to other professionals in the community.

5	5	**12.** One response is required. Answers will depend on the provider, the children in her care, and the families. Generally, responses should indicate that the provider:

- Is aware of family members' feelings and ideas,
- Is willing to apologize when appropriate,
- Sees conflicts with families as a normal part of sharing care of a child,
- Can see the situation from the family's perspective,
- Can explain her perspective to the family, and
- Keeps the child's interests in the forefront.

5	5	**13.** Two responses are required. There are numerous possible answers. Examples of correct responses include the following:

- Family members' extended deployment.
- Illness or death of family member or close relative.
- Separation or divorce.
- Financial difficulties.
- Unplanned or unwanted pregnancy.
- Feelings of isolation.

Module 12: Program Management

Total of 100 points possible. Passing score is 80 or above.

Each Answer Worth	Possible Total Points	**Answer**
2 1/2	2 1/2	**1.** e
2 1/2	2 1/2	**2.** c
5	5	**3.** Evaluate the program. As a provider plans and implements her program, she needs to evaluate its effectiveness.

5 ea.	15	**4.**	Three responses are required. Examples of correct responses include the following:

- To plan a program that meets each child's needs, interests, and strengths.
- To develop a strategy for dealing with a challenging behavior.
- To collect information to share with others who care for the child, especially families.
- To evaluate an activity, the environment, or a particular toy or piece of equipment.

5	5	**5.**	The provider's system for observation should allow her to record frequent, brief (3- to 5-minute) observations of all the children in the group, at different times of the day, over time. Review Learning Activity I, Using a Systematic Approach to Observing and Taking Notes, to see if the provider has incorporated any of the suggested strategies in her system.

5	5	**6.**	Objectivity and accuracy. The provider needs to make sure her observations of children's behavior are objective and accurate and not her interpretations or judgments.

5	5	**7.**	Examples of correct response includes the following:

Evaluation allows providers to determine whether:
- Activity goals were met.
- How her practices can be improved.
- An activity or routine should occur more frequently.
- Which children enjoyed and learned from an activity or routine.

10	10	**8.**	An objective and accurate rewrite such as the following would be a correct response.

Germaine (11 months) crawled quickly over to Brett (12 months). She took a toy from his hand. He cried.

2 1/2 ea.	30	**9.**	Twelve responses are required, two for each category. Responses will depend on the provider, the children, the environment, and so on. The following examples for each category should help you score the provider's responses:

a. Changes to the environment: Adding or rotating toys, materials, or equipment; decorating walls; storing and displaying materials; moving furniture; and so on.

b. Special activity: Neighborhood walk, food preparation, introducing a new piece of equipment, putting out a prop box, and so on.

c. Changes to daily routines: At lunch, serve and talk about the zucchini we grew in our garden and then prepared together.

d. Family involvement: Ask families to tell me about their experiences while cooking with children, to give me ideas for cooking activities.

e. To do: Look through cookbooks for some simple zucchini recipes. Fill lidded containers with fresh tempera paint.

184

| 5 ea. | 10 | **10.** | Two responses are required. Obtain copies of the FCC program's policies and procedures and use them to determine if the provider's policies and procedures are appropriate and clearly explained. |
| 5 ea. | 10 | **11.** | Provider should include two strategies in her response. There are many correct responses. Judge whether provider uses effective managerial strategies. Give full credit for complete response. |

Module 13: Professionalism

Total of 100 points possible. Passing score is 80 or above.

Each Answer Worth	Possible Total Points		**Answer**
2 1/2	2 1/2	**1.**	d
2 1/2	2 1/2	**2.**	d
2 1/2 ea.	7.5	**3.**	a (2) b (3) c (1)
1 ea.	5	**4**	c, d, f, g, h
5 ea.	10	**5.**	Two responses are required. Use your own judgment to score this question. Refer to Learning Activity II, Continuing to Learn About Caring for Children, for guidance.
5	5	**6.**	Responses will vary according to provider's goals. Appropriate responses are those that make positive statements about professional growth and show provider is confident about herself and her progress.
5 ea.	10	**7.**	Two responses are required. Use your own judgment to score this question. Refer to Learning Activity IV, Becoming an Advocate for Children and Families, for guidance.
5 ea.	10	**8.**	Two responses are required. Examples of correct responses include the following:

- There are always new developments in the field.
- Continued learning brings new ideas to the job.
- She cares about children and wants to meet their needs in the best ways possible.
- She wants to take on more responsibility, share her experience and knowledge, and perhaps earn a higher salary.

| 2 1/2 ea. | 10 | **9.** | Four responses are required. Provider's answers will vary according to her experience, education, and interests. Responses should reflect provider's understanding of the skills and knowledge of the profession. Use you own judgment to score this question. |
| 5 ea. | 20 | **10.** | One response is required for each of the four categories. Provider's answers will vary, so use your judgment to score this question. |

10   10   **11.** Discuss the provider's thoughts about early childhood education as a career and assist her in planning ways to increase experience and knowledge. All appropriate answers should receive 10 points.

2 1/2 ea.   7.5   **12.** Three responses are required. Provider may list any of the 13 CDA Functional Areas (Safe, Healthy, Learning Environment, Physical, Cognitive, Communication, Creative, Self, Social, Guidance, Families, Program Management, and Professionalism).

Appendix C

Trainer Observation Forms for Competency Assessments

MODULE 1: SAFE[*]

Provider: _____   **Observer:** _____

Date/time: _____   **Setting:** _____

Observation Record: _____

_____

_____

_____

_____

_____

_____

_____

_____

_____

_____

_____

_____

_____

_____

_____

_____

_____

* This competency assessment must include observation of an emergency drill.

MODULE 1: SAFE (continued)

MODULE 1: SAFE (continued)

Before the observation period, assess the following criteria.

THE COMPETENT PROVIDER WILL:

Conduct daily and monthly safety checks indoors and outdoors and remove or repair unsafe items.
[ ] met　　[ ] partially met　　[ ] not met

Arrange the FCC home so there are clear exits.
[ ] met　　[ ] partially met　　[ ] not met

Organize indoor and outdoor areas so children can move freely without bumping into things.
[ ] met　　[ ] partially met　　[ ] not met

Provide safe, age-appropriate toys, materials, equipment, and activities.
[ ] met　　[ ] partially met　　[ ] not met

Arrange toys on low, open shelves with the heaviest items on the bottom shelves.
[ ] met　　[ ] partially met　　[ ] not met

Maintain a fully stocked first-aid kit.
[ ] met　　[ ] partially met　　[ ] not met

State the correct procedures to follow when there is an injury or emergency.
[ ] met　　[ ] partially met　　[ ] not met

Maintain up-to-date emergency telephone numbers for all families.
[ ] met　　[ ] partially met　　[ ] not met

Post emergency phone numbers for children's families, police, fire, ambulance, and poison control next to the telephone.
[ ] met　　[ ] partially met　　[ ] not met

Keep electrical wires in good condition and out of children's reach.
[ ] met　　[ ] partially met　　[ ] not met

Store breakable items out of children's reach.
[ ] met　　[ ] partially met　　[ ] not met

Review your observation record and score each criterion of competence that you can substantiate from this observation.

THE COMPETENT PROVIDER WILL

Conduct and document monthly emergency drills and notify the families after they take place.
[ ] met　　[ ] partially met　　[ ] not met

Show children the FCC home is a safe place and that keeping them safe is important.
[ ] met　　[ ] partially met　　[ ] not met

Respond quickly to children in distress.
[ ] met　　[ ] partially met　　[ ] not met

Follow a daily schedule that provides time for active and quiet play so that children do not get injured because they are overtired.
[ ] met　　[ ] partially met　　[ ] not met

Take precautions in a reassuring way without overprotecting or scaring children.
[ ] met　　[ ] partially met　　[ ] not met

Use diagrams, pictures, and words to remind children of safety rules.
[ ] met　　[ ] partially met　　[ ] not met

Model ways to live safely and be careful throughout the day.
[ ] met　　[ ] partially met　　[ ] not met

Use positive guidance to redirect children from unsafe to safe activities.
[ ] met　　[ ] partially met　　[ ] not met

Keep small, easily swallowed objects out of the reach of young children.
[ ] met　　[ ] partially met　　[ ] not met

MODULE 2: HEALTHY

Provider: _____   **Observer:** _____

Date/time: _____   **Setting:** _____

Observation Record:

MODULE 2: HEALTHY (continued)

MODULE 2: HEALTHY (continued)

Prior to the observation period, assess the following criteria.

THE COMPETENT PROVIDER WILL:

Check the home daily for adequate ventilation and lighting, comfortable room temperature, and good sanitation.
[ ] met   [ ] partially met   [ ] not met

Place tissues, paper towels, and soap within children's reach.
[ ] met   [ ] partially met   [ ] not met

Arrange the diaper area and/or the bathroom so it is easy to keep sanitary.
[ ] met   [ ] partially met   [ ] not met

Provide a place to isolate an ill child until the family member arrives.
[ ] met   [ ] partially met   [ ] not met

Explain the applicable laws and regulations related to reporting child abuse and neglect, and describe the signs of possible child abuse and neglect.
[ ] met   [ ] partially met   [ ] not met

Review your observation record and score each criterion of competence that you can substantiate from this observation.

THE COMPETENT PROVIDER WILL:

Open windows daily to let in fresh air (if needed during observation period).
[ ] met   [ ] partially met   [ ] not met

Clean and disinfect surfaces before and after food preparation.
[ ] met   [ ] partially met   [ ] not met

Wash hands with soap and water before children arrive, before and after eating, before and after food preparation, before and after diapering or toileting a child, after wiping a child's nose, and as necessary.
[ ] met   [ ] partially met   [ ] not met

Wash children's hands (or help them do it themselves) with soap and water upon arrival, before and after eating, before participating in a food preparation activity, after toileting or diapering, after wiping noses, and as necessary.
[ ] met   [ ] partially met   [ ] not met

Wash and disinfect with bleach solution toys that are mouthed or fall on the floor (at least daily).
[ ] met   [ ] partially met   [ ] not met

Serve age-appropriate, healthy foods that are low in fats, salt, and sugar and meet Child and Adult Care Food Program requirements.
[ ] met   [ ] partially met   [ ] not met

Serve relaxed, family-style meals and encourage children to try new foods.
[ ] met   [ ] partially met   [ ] not met

Hold and talk to infants while feeding them.
[ ] met   [ ] partially met   [ ] not met

Help children learn self-help skills (toileting, feeding, toothbrushing, etc.).
[ ] met   [ ] partially met   [ ] not met

Talk with children about ways to stay healthy.
[ ] met   [ ] partially met   [ ] not met

Provide a balanced schedule so children get enough exercise and rest.
[ ] met   [ ] partially met   [ ] not met

Take children outdoors every day.
[ ] met   [ ] partially met   [ ] not met

Refrigerate infant bottles and foods in individual, labeled containers and discard unused portions.
[ ] met   [ ] partially met   [ ] not met

Store food properly, in dated containers.
[ ] met   [ ] partially met   [ ] not met

Maintain a positive, relaxed atmosphere to reduce tension and stress.
[ ] met   [ ] partially met   [ ] not met

MODULE 3: LEARNING ENVIRONMENT

Provider: _____

Observer: _____

Date/time: _____

Setting: _____

Observation Record: _____

MODULE 3: LEARNING ENVIRONMENT (continued)

MODULE 3: LEARNING ENVIRONMENT (continued)

Prior to the observation period, assess the following criteria.

THE COMPETENT PROVIDER WILL:

Set up a welcoming environment with spaces for a variety of activities.
[ ] met   [ ] partially met   [ ] not met

Provide cozy spaces (indoors and outdoors) where children can be alone.
[ ] met   [ ] partially met   [ ] not met

Provide open areas with a variety of surfaces for children to explore.
[ ] met   [ ] partially met   [ ] not met

Arrange indoor and outdoor areas where children can use their large muscles.
[ ] met   [ ] partially met   [ ] not met

Have child-size furniture and equipment for children to use.
[ ] met   [ ] partially met   [ ] not met

Adapt the environment, if needed, for children with special needs.
[ ] met   [ ] partially met   [ ] not met

Plan a consistent, flexible schedule with daily opportunities for indoor and outdoor experiences.
[ ] met   [ ] partially met   [ ] not met

Review your observation record and score each criterion of competence that you can substantiate from this observation.

THE COMPETENT PROVIDER WILL:

Include toys and activities that correspond to a variety of ethnicities and cultures, including those of the children in her care.
[ ] met   [ ] partially met   [ ] not met

Convey positive messages through the arrangement of the environment (e.g., "This is a safe place.").
[ ] met   [ ] partially met   [ ] not met

Arrange materials so children have clear choices and are encouraged to be independent.
[ ] met   [ ] partially met   [ ] not met

Provide materials and equipment that provide challenges and allow children to be successful.
[ ] met   [ ] partially met   [ ] not met

Provide materials that are appropriate for the interests and abilities of the children in her care.
[ ] met   [ ] partially met   [ ] not met

Provide a variety of materials to encourage development in all areas.
[ ] met   [ ] partially met   [ ] not met

Adapt the schedule to meet children's individual needs.
[ ] met   [ ] partially met   [ ] not met

Adapt the schedule to take advantage of unscheduled learning opportunities.
[ ] met   [ ] partially met   [ ] not met

Allow ample time for daily routines and use them as opportunities for learning.
[ ] met   [ ] partially met   [ ] not met

Make sure all the children can be seen at all times.
[ ] met   [ ] partially met   [ ] not met

MODULE 4: PHYSICAL

Provider: _____

Observer: _____

Date/time: _____

Setting: _____

Observation Record: _____

MODULE 4: PHYSICAL (continued)

MODULE 4: PHYSICAL (continued)

During the observation period, assess the following criteria.

THE COMPETENT PROVIDER WILL:

Schedule time for the children to engage in active play every day.
[ ] met   [ ] partially met   [ ] not met

Help and encourage children when they are learning new skills.
[ ] met   [ ] partially met   [ ] not met

Provide safe and interesting objects for children to listen to, taste, smell, look at, and handle.
[ ] met   [ ] partially met   [ ] not met

Observe and record information about each child's physical strengths, interests, and needs.
[ ] met   [ ] partially met   [ ] not met

Help children develop an awareness of rhythm through music and movement.
[ ] met   [ ] partially met   [ ] not met

Arrange the indoor and outdoor environment so children can move freely and safely.
[ ] met   [ ] partially met   [ ] not met

Offer a variety of materials and equipment to promote gross motor skills.
[ ] met   [ ] partially met   [ ] not met

Play indoor and outdoor noncompetitive games with children.
[ ] met   [ ] partially met   [ ] not met

Encourage the development of self-help skills that use gross motor skills.
[ ] met   [ ] partially met   [ ] not met

Plan and implement increasingly difficult activities in which gross motor skills are used.
[ ] met   [ ] partially met   [ ] not met

Decide when to intervene directly and when to let a child work out a problem.
[ ] met   [ ] partially met   [ ] not met

Offer a variety of materials that promote fine motor skills.
[ ] met   [ ] partially met   [ ] not met

Provide opportunities for children to develop fine motor skills such as grasping, throwing, catching, rolling, squeezing, dropping, pounding, pulling, zipping, spreading, pouring, twisting, and buttoning.
[ ] met   [ ] partially met   [ ] not met

Plan and implement increasingly difficult activities in which fine motor skills are used.
[ ] met   [ ] partially met   [ ] not met

Encourage children to participate in daily routines such as setting the tables for meals, wiping up spills, and sweeping sand.
[ ] met   [ ] partially met   [ ] not met

MODULE 5: COGNITIVE

Provider: _____   **Observer:** _____

Date/time: _____   **Setting:** _____

Observation Record: _____

MODULE 5: COGNITIVE (continued)

MODULE 5: COGNITIVE (continued)

During the observation period, assess the following criteria.

THE COMPETENT PROVIDER WILL:

Use information gained through observations to support individual children's learning.
[ ] met   [ ] partially met   [ ] not met

Provide experiences and activities that allow children to use and refine their senses (touching, tasting, hearing, smelling, and seeing).
[ ] met   [ ] partially met   [ ] not met

Talk to children about what they are doing, thinking, and feeling.
[ ] met   [ ] partially met   [ ] not met

Provide a variety of open-ended materials that can be explored and used in different ways by children of different ages.
[ ] met   [ ] partially met   [ ] not met

Provide toys, materials, and activities that are challenging but allow children to be successful.
[ ] met   [ ] partially met   [ ] not met

Provide opportunities for children to learn about similarities and differences, object permanence, cause and effect, making predictions, and solving problems.
[ ] met   [ ] partially met   [ ] not met

Use open-ended prompts that encourage children to think.
[ ] met   [ ] partially met   [ ] not met

Respect children's questions and respond in ways that promote thinking skills.
[ ] met   [ ] partially met   [ ] not met

Provide assistance when children seem to need an adult's help.
[ ] met   [ ] partially met   [ ] not met

Allow children to solve their own problems when they don't seem to need an adult's help.
[ ] met   [ ] partially met   [ ] not met

Use daily routines and household objects for learning.
[ ] met   [ ] partially met   [ ] not met

Provide materials and encourage older children to pursue projects and hobbies.
[ ] met   [ ] partially met   [ ] not met

Answer children's questions and encourage them to continue asking questions.
[ ] met   [ ] partially met   [ ] not met

Show respect for and interest in children's ideas and feelings.
[ ] met   [ ] partially met   [ ] not met

Talk to children about what she and they are doing, during daily routines (for example, "I see you have little goose bumps on your arm, and I think you might be cold—let's put your sweater on.").
[ ] met   [ ] partially met   [ ] not met

MODULE 6: COMMUNICATION

Provider: _____

Observer: _____

Date/time: _____

Setting: _____

Observation Record: _____

MODULE 6: COMMUNICATION (continued)

MODULE 6: COMMUNICATION (continued)

During the observation period, assess the following criteria.

THE COMPETENT PROVIDER WILL:

Pay attention to children's verbal and nonverbal communication and help them express their ideas and feelings (for example, "You look like you had a hard day at school. Would you like to talk about it?").
[ ] met   [ ] partially met   [ ] not met

Respond to infants' vocalizations—gurgling, cooing, crying, whimpering—by smiling and talking to them.
[ ] met   [ ] partially met   [ ] not met

Encourage children to communicate with each other verbally.
[ ] met   [ ] partially met   [ ] not met

Accept children's way of speaking.
[ ] met   [ ] partially met   [ ] not met

Serve as a language model.
[ ] met   [ ] partially met   [ ] not met

Converse with children about their feelings, ideas, and activities.
[ ] met   [ ] partially met   [ ] not met

Listen attentively to what children say and respect their ideas.
[ ] met   [ ] partially met   [ ] not met

Play games, such as finger plays, to encourage children to talk and sing.
[ ] met   [ ] partially met   [ ] not met

Provide safe and inviting places for children to talk and play together.
[ ] met   [ ] partially met   [ ] not met

Provide props and support children's pretend and dramatic play.
[ ] met   [ ] partially met   [ ] not met

Provide books that correspond to children's interests and levels of development.
[ ] met   [ ] partially met   [ ] not met

Display books attractively.
[ ] met   [ ] partially met   [ ] not met

Provide quiet, cozy places for looking at books and reading.
[ ] met   [ ] partially met   [ ] not met

Read books with children every day.
[ ] met   [ ] partially met   [ ] not met

Provide a wide variety of paper and writing tools to encourage children to scribble and write.
[ ] met   [ ] partially met   [ ] not met

Model writing and reading as a part of daily activities.
[ ] met   [ ] partially met   [ ] not met

Use words and phrases from the children's home languages.
[ ] met   [ ] partially met   [ ] not met

MODULE 7: CREATIVE

Provider: _____   Observer: _____

Date/time: _____   Setting: _____

Observation Record: _____

MODULE 7: CREATIVE (continued)

MODULE 7: CREATVE (continued)

During the observation period, assess the following criteria.

THE COMPETENT PROVIDER WILL:

Arrange the environment so that children can easily select, replace, and care for materials and equipment.
[ ] met   [ ] partially met   [ ] not met

Provide the space and time children need to explore, use their imaginations, make plans, and carry them out.
[ ] met   [ ] partially met   [ ] not met

Provide sufficient space for children's ongoing projects.
[ ] met   [ ] partially met   [ ] not met

Offer sensory experiences ("Smell the spices we are going to use in the muffins.").
[ ] met   [ ] partially met   [ ] not met

Provide toys, materials, and activities (for example, blocks, sand and water play, plastic bowls and lids, a wagon) that children can use in different ways.
[ ] met   [ ] partially met   [ ] not met

Provide dress-up clothes and props for pretend and dramatic play, and participate in children's dramatic play.
[ ] met   [ ] partially met   [ ] not met

Provide a variety of art materials that children may use for their own creations.
[ ] met   [ ] partially met   [ ] not met

Conduct a variety of planned and spontaneous music and movement activities.
[ ] met   [ ] partially met   [ ] not met

Establish a secure and trusting relationship with each child.
[ ] met   [ ] partially met   [ ] not met

Acknowledge children's creative thinking (for example, "You opened both ends of the box. Now you can crawl through.").
[ ] met   [ ] partially met   [ ] not met

Support children to enable them to solve their own problems.
[ ] met   [ ] partially met   [ ] not met

Respond to younger children in ways that acknowledge their interest in the process of creating rather than the product of their efforts.
[ ] met   [ ] partially met   [ ] not met

Respond to older children in ways that acknowledge that they care about the products that result from their creative endeavors.
[ ] met   [ ] partially met   [ ] not met

Use open-ended prompts that encourage creative thinking.
[ ] met   [ ] partially met   [ ] not met

Show respect for children's creativity by waiting until they are finished before asking them to do something else.
[ ] met   [ ] partially met   [ ] not met

MODULE 8: SELF

Provider: _____

Date/time: _____

Observation Record: _____

Observer: _____

Setting: _____

Page 1

210

MODULE 8: SELF (continued)

211

MODULE 8: SELF (continued)

During the observation period, assess the following criteria.

THE COMPETENT PROVIDER WILL:

Plan the day's activities and provide materials that reflect children's needs, interests, and strengths.
[ ] met   [ ] partially met   [ ] not met

Display pictures of families and provide space for personal belongings.
[ ] met   [ ] partially met   [ ] not met

Talk with children about their feelings so they can understand and express their emotions.
[ ] met   [ ] partially met   [ ] not met

Help children make the transition from their homes to the FCC home.
[ ] met   [ ] partially met   [ ] not met

Give individual attention to each child every day.
[ ] met   [ ] partially met   [ ] not met

Let children know that she values them even when they have negative emotions or cannot control their behavior.
[ ] met   [ ] partially met   [ ] not met

Show children in many ways that their well-being is important to her.
[ ] met   [ ] partially met   [ ] not met

Use language and actions to express pleasure and interest in individual children and what they are doing.
[ ] met   [ ] partially met   [ ] not met

Help children learn to use language and to let each other know what they want and feel.
[ ] met   [ ] partially met   [ ] not met

Model positive ways to talk and act to show other people that she cares about them.
[ ] met   [ ] partially met   [ ] not met

Allow and encourage children to make choices (for example, what to eat at snack time or what materials to use).
[ ] met   [ ] partially met   [ ] not met

Offer help to children when they are learning new skills.
[ ] met   [ ] partially met   [ ] not met

Allow children to learn from their mistakes and support them as they try to solve their own problems.
[ ] met   [ ] partially met   [ ] not met

Repeat activities so children can practice and master new skills.
[ ] met   [ ] partially met   [ ] not met

Let children do as much as possible for themselves and each other; provide help only when it is requested or needed.
[ ] met   [ ] partially met   [ ] not met

MODULE 9: SOCIAL

Provider: _____

Date/time: _____

Observation Record: _____

Observer: _____

Setting: _____

MODULE 9: SOCIAL (continued)

MODULE 9: SOCIAL (continued)

During the observation period, assess the following criteria.

THE COMPETENT PROVIDER WILL:

Observe to learn how each child relates to the others in her care.
[ ] met   [ ] partially met   [ ] not met

Talk, make eye contact, and play with children to give them experience in interacting with another person.
[ ] met   [ ] partially met   [ ] not met

Encourage children to help each other.
[ ] met   [ ] partially met   [ ] not met

Support children to enable them to solve their own conflicts.
[ ] met   [ ] partially met   [ ] not met

Model positive ways to cooperate, share, and interact with others.
[ ] met   [ ] partially met   [ ] not met

Provide materials and activities that can involve more than one child at a time.
[ ] met   [ ] partially met   [ ] not met

Help younger children learn to express their feelings verbally, and remind older children to tell others how they feel.
[ ] met   [ ] partially met   [ ] not met

Provide a variety of props so children can use pretend and dramatic play to manage their feelings and explore social roles.
[ ] met   [ ] partially met   [ ] not met

Express her own feelings when appropriate so children can learn to express their feelings.
[ ] met   [ ] partially met   [ ] not met

Verbalize what children may be feeling but are unable to express.
[ ] met   [ ] partially met   [ ] not met

Meet young children's needs according to their personal schedules for eating, sleeping, toileting, and so on.
[ ] met   [ ] partially met   [ ] not met

Talk with children about what they are doing, to show her respect and appreciation for their efforts.
[ ] met   [ ] partially met   [ ] not met

Arrange the environment so children can be alone or with one or two others.
[ ] met   [ ] partially met   [ ] not met

Plan special group projects such as painting a mural so children of different ages can play and work together.
[ ] met   [ ] partially met   [ ] not met

Provide duplicates of favorite toys so children can play together without having to share before they are developmentally ready.
[ ] met   [ ] partially met   [ ] not met

Create prop boxes with materials related to children's interests and that can be used for pretend and dramatic play by children of different ages.
[ ] met   [ ] partially met   [ ] not met

Provide duplicates of certain dramatic play props, such as firefighter hats, to encourage group play.
[ ] met   [ ] partially met   [ ] not met

Provide some toys and materials, such as beads and string, that children may use when they want to play alone.
[ ] met   [ ] partially met   [ ] not met

MODULE 10: GUIDANCE

Provider: _____

Observer: _____

Date/time: _____

Setting: _____

Observation Record: _____

MODULE 10: GUIDANCE (continued)

217

MODULE 10: GUIDANCE (continued)

Prior to the observation period, assess the following criteria.

THE COMPETENT PROVIDER WILL:

Remove hazards so children can safely play and explore.
[ ] met   [ ] partially met   [ ] not met

Provide storage places with picture and word labels to show where things go.
[ ] met   [ ] partially met   [ ] not met

Keep toys and other safe materials on low, open shelves so children can help themselves.
[ ] met   [ ] partially met   [ ] not met

Provide a place for older children to store their toys and materials out of the reach of the younger children.
[ ] met   [ ] partially met   [ ] not met

Provide a balanced daily schedule with time for both active and quite play, indoors and outdoors.
[ ] met   [ ] partially met   [ ] not met

Review your observation record and score each criterion of competence that you can substantiate from this observation.

THE COMPETENT PROVIDER WILL:

Provide a variety of materials and activities to meet children's needs, strengths and interests.
[ ] met   [ ] partially met   [ ] not met

Provide sufficient developmentally appropriate materials for the children in the home, including duplicates of popular items.
[ ] met   [ ] partially met   [ ] not met

Involve children in setting limits and making rules for the FCC home.
[ ] met   [ ] partially met   [ ] not met

Try to understand the reasons for children's behavior.
[ ] met   [ ] partially met   [ ] not met

Help children to use their problem-solving skills to resolve conflicts.
[ ] met   [ ] partially met   [ ] not met

Give directions and remind children of the rules in positive ways (e.g., "walk in the house").
[ ] met   [ ] partially met   [ ] not met

Reinforce children's positive behavior with meaningful comments.
[ ] met   [ ] partially met   [ ] not met

Give children opportunities to make developmentally apporopriate, meaningful choices.
[ ] met   [ ] partially met   [ ] not met

Model appropriate ways to express feelings.
[ ] met   [ ] partially met   [ ] not met

Provide soothing activities such as playdough, water play, or simple crafts, and redirect upset children to these activities.
[ ] met   [ ] partially met   [ ] not met

Talk to school-age children about their day at school, their friends, their concerns, and so on.
[ ] met   [ ] partially met   [ ] not met

Remind children to use words to tell others how they feel.
[ ] met   [ ] partially met   [ ] not met

Work with families to help children express feelings in acceptable ways.
[ ] met   [ ] partially met   [ ] not met

MODULE 11: FAMILIES

Page 1

Provider: _____   Observer: _____

Date/time: _____   Setting: _____

Observation Record: _____

MODULE 11: FAMILIES (continued)

MODULE 11: FAMILIES (continued)

During the observation period, assess the following criteria.

THE COMPETENT PROVIDER WILL:

Share with families information about their child's day—feedings or meal times, naps, play, and interactions.
[ ] met   [ ] partially met   [ ] not met

Help parents understand what their child learns through everyday activities.
[ ] met   [ ] partially met   [ ] not met

Share with families some good news about their child's day.
[ ] met   [ ] partially met   [ ] not met

Listen when families share information about their child.
[ ] met   [ ] partially met   [ ] not met

Involve families in making decisions about their child's care.
[ ] met   [ ] partially met   [ ] not met

Suggest ways to support learning at home.
[ ] met   [ ] partially met   [ ] not met

Respond to families' questions and concerns about their child's development, and share in their delight.
[ ] met   [ ] partially met   [ ] not met

Work with families to guide children's behavior and respond to their strengths and needs.
[ ] met   [ ] partially met   [ ] not met

Share information with parents about current activities and future plans at the FCC home.
[ ] met   [ ] partially met   [ ] not met

Help families participate and be involved in the program.
[ ] met   [ ] partially met   [ ] not met

Help families understand the reasons for their child's behavior.
[ ] met   [ ] partially met   [ ] not met

Provide support for families under stress (if an opportunity arises during the observation period).
[ ] met   [ ] partially met   [ ] not met

Appendix D

Tracking Forms

Individual Tracking Form

Name: _____

Indicate date completed

Module	Over-view	Pre-training Assess-ment	L.A. I	L.A. II	L.A. III	L.A. IV	L.A. V	L.A. VI	Know-ledge Assess-ment	Comp-tency Assess-ment	Trainer Sign-off
1. Safe											
2. Healthy								░			
3. Learning Environment							░	░			
4. Physical								░			
5. Cognitive								░			
6. Communication								░			
7. Creative							░	░			
8. Self											
9. Social								░			
10. Guidance								░			
11. Families											
12. Program Management							░	░		░	
13. Professionalism								░		░	

Key
Shaded areas indicate that particular learning activities and the competency assessment are **not** included in a module.

Group Tracking Form

MODULES

PROVIDERS	Intro		1		2		3		4		5		6		7		8		9		10		11		12		13	
	B	C	B	C	B	C	B	C	B	C	B	C	B	C	B	C	B	C	B	C	B	C	B	C	B	C	B	C

Provider Programs:

B=Begun
C=Completed

Modules:

Intro=Introduction
1=Safe
2=Healthy
3=Learning Environment
4=Physical

5=Cognitive
6=Communication
7=Creative
8=Self
9=Social

10=Guidance
11=Families
12=Program Management
13=Professionalism

LEGEND

227

Appendix E

Documentation of Training Hours

DOCUMENTATION OF TRAINING

Provider's name _____

Topic (NAFCC Accreditation, CDA Functional Area, or Licensing Requirement)	Date of Training or Observation	Number of Hours	Type of Training (conference, course, workshop, observation/feedback)	Agency Providing Training Signature of Trainer

232

Appendix F

Certificate of Completion

CERTIFICATE of COMPLETION

AWARDED TO

_____

for completion of _____ hours of training

on *Caring for Children in Family Child Care*

_____ 20 ___

Verification of Training may be obtained from:

Agency Sponsoring Training: _____

Sponsor's Address: _____

City/State/Zip: _____

Sponsor's Phone Number: (___) _____

_____

(Trainer's Signature)